JAYNE TORVILL

&

CHRISTOPHER DEAN

Ice Dancing's Perfect Pair

Franny Shuker-Haines

B L A C K B I R C H   P R E S S

W O O D B R I D G E ,   C O N N E C T I C U T

Published by Blackbirch Press, Inc.
One Bradley Road
Woodbridge, CT 06525

Printed in Canada

10 9 8 7 6 5 4 3 2 1

Photo Credits

Cover: ©Syndication International Ltd.; p. 4: ©Syndication International Ltd.; p. 37: ©The Hulton-Deutsch Collection; p. 42: ©Syndication International Ltd.; p. 59: ©The Hulton-Deutsch Collection; p. 77: UPI/Bettmann; p. 78: UPI/Bettmann; p. 85: ©Syndication International Ltd.; p. 92: ©Mark Allan/Globe Photos, Inc.; p. 101: Reuters/Bettmann; p. 103: ©Dave Parker/Globe Photos, Inc.

Library of Congress Cataloging-in-Publication Data

Shuker-Haines, Franny.
    Torvill & Dean, ice dancing's perfect pair / by Franny Shuker-Haines.
— 1st ed.
        p. cm. — Partners
    Includes bibliographical references (p.) and index.
    ISBN 1-56711-134-3 (lib. bdg.)
    1. Torvill, Jayne, 1957- —Juvenile literature. 2. Dean, Christopher, 1958- —Juvenile literature. 3. Skaters—Great Britain—Biography—Juvenile literature. 4. Ice dancing—Great Britain—Juvenile literature. I. Title. II. Title: Torvill and Dean, ice dancing's perfect pair. III. Series
GV850.T63S48   1995
796.91'2—dc20   94-46684
                                                                              CIP
                                                                              AC

Table of Contents

With their unique blend of artistry and technical excellence, Jayne Torvill and Christopher Dean single-handedly raised the standards of ice dancing.

Art on Ice

Torvill and Dean have

changed the world

of ice dancing.

Imagine a British bobby, strolling along the streets of Nottingham, England, writing a few tickets, making an arrest for disorderly conduct outside a pub, helping a lost child find the way home. Then imagine him hanging up his uniform, cap, and stick after a long, exhausting day and heading over to the ice-skating rink to lace up his skates and practice the rumba for another three hours before he can fall into bed.

Imagine, too, a mild-mannered British secretary processing insurance claims all day long in a large corporation. She is a typical office worker—except that at the end of every day, while her co-workers are hurrying home or going out to the movies, she is still not done. But this time she is at the ice rink, where she goes to practice, practice, practice until every single step of her latest ice-dancing routine is exactly right.

Now imagine that these two unlikely souls together would become the most important, influential, and perfect ice dancers ever. Once you do that, you may have some idea of the extraordinary story of Olympic champions Jayne Torvill and Christopher Dean.

Torvill and Dean, Chris and Jayne, T & D—by whatever name that you know them—are probably best remembered for their remarkable performance at the 1984 Winter Olympics at Sarajevo in the former Yugoslavia. There, they performed their four-and-a-half minute free-dance routine to Ravel's "Bolero," a sensuous, driving piece of music that starts out slow and sultry, gradually becoming more intense and urgent. It has a relentless beat with a haunting melody and tension as it builds and climbs to a dramatic, sudden end. Torvill and Dean, dressed in shades of purple, began the routine on their knees, swaying gently to the music. Then they gradually moved up and out, covering the ice with one of the most romantic, sensuous, beautiful, inventive, and technically perfect performances ever executed on ice. They brought down the house, and for their efforts, they received terrific scores: six 5.9s and three 6.0s (out of a perfect 6.0) for technical merit and nine perfect 6.0s for artistic impression. It was an Olympic first, it has never been repeated.

In the course of their competitive career, Torvill and Dean amassed more perfect scores than any other ice-dancing couple. They won the British Ice-Dancing Championships seven times, the European Championships four times, and were world champions for four consecutive years. Winning an Olympic gold medal in 1984, they returned ten years later to Olympic competition to capture the bronze. The combination of technical perfection, innovative choreography, and a sensitivity to music that they brought to the ice changed the sport forever. Many have said that Torvill and Dean moved ice dancing from the world of sport to the world of art, emphasizing dance over skating, and using the speed and freedom of the ice to give dance a new fluidity and exhilaration. Their rise from Saturdays spent goofing around with friends at the ice rink in Nottingham, England, to the pinnacle of Olympic competition and beyond is a triumph of hard work. It is also an achievement that represents a true blending of two distinct personalities and skills to create a seamless union of technique and artistic expression.

Finding Each Other

"No one works harder than Torvill and

Dean. Not me. Not anyone."

—Scott Hamilton , U.S. Olympic
Skating Champion

Jayne Torvill was born on October 7, 1957. An only child, she grew up living over her parents' newsstand in Nottingham, England. Unlike the many athletes who start training at age three and are burned-out by age twelve, Jayne didn't even put on skates until she was nine years old. A teacher at her school organized a class skating trip, and Jayne had a great time on the ice. Afterwards, she began pestering her parents for skates and soon received a second-hand pair. She loved skating so much that, often, when it was time for her to go home, she would hide in the middle of the swirl of skaters making it impossible for her parents to see her, much less reach her!

9

Christopher Dean's ice-skating start was equally unceremonious. He was born July 27, 1958. His father was a Coal Board electrician, and the family lived just outside Nottingham. When Christopher was ten, his mother decided he should have an interest outside of school, one that would keep him busy and take him into town more often. Because his mother had done some skating when she was young, she thought that her only son might enjoy it, too. That year Christopher received a pair of skates for Christmas and started spending his free time at the ice rink in Nottingham. Unaware of each other's existence, Jayne and Chris shared the ice as children, honing their skills and a love for the sport among the chatting families and first-time skaters at the public skating rink.

Jayne quickly became good enough to skate competitively. She started her career in pairs and solo skating, rather than ice dancing. What separates these forms of figure skating is the word "dancing." Rooted in the art of ballroom dancing, ice dancing emphasizes skating in couples to traditional ballroom music. All aspects of ice-dancing competition are determined by the musical form and the type of dancing that goes with it. Just as ballroom dancers might dance a tango—a predetermined set of steps combined, perhaps, in creative ways—to a piece of music called a "tango," ice dancers also perform a predetermined set of steps to particular kinds of music (at least for part of a competition). A competitive ice-dancing couple—and it is always a couple; there is no solo ice dancing—must complete three "sets" of dances for each competition. First come the "compulsories." Each year, the International Skating Union (ISU) establishes which types of music will be used for the compulsory dances and the steps that must be included. Each couple must perform the very same dance to the very same music throughout that year's tournaments. There are two compulsories for each competition, a waltz and a rumba, for example, or blues and rock-and-roll. Compulsories allow the judges to evaluate couples on technique alone. A couple's scores at this level will establish their standing in the competition as they go into the next round.

The second tier of an ice-dancing competition is the short program (formerly called the Original Set Pattern, or OSP, and now called the Original Program). This is a two- to two-and-a-half-minute routine of original choreography skated to a predetermined type of dance music. The skaters may, for example, pick any version of a Westminster waltz and skate to it in any creative way they choose—as long as they remain within the bounds of the strict rules of ice dancing.

These strict rules are another way in which ice dancing differs from other forms of figure skating. Ice dancers are expected to dance together for almost their entire program. They may separate only a certain number of times, and then only for five seconds at a time. They are not permitted to spin or perform large jumps. The man may not lift the woman above his shoulders, and when he does lift her, he may do so only a few times per dance. While these rules may seem ridiculously stifling to a casual observer, they are meant to distinguish ice dancing from pairs skating. Ice dancing is about seamless unity on the ice, two people skating as one, dancing to music in a disciplined yet seemingly effortless way.

After the short program comes the most expressive of the ice dancers' competitive routines—the four- to four-and-a-half-minute "Free Dance." Here, the skaters may choose their own music and skate to it in any way they like (again, without breaking any of the rules). For the many years leading up to the reign of Torvill and Dean, couples would choose four distinct tempos for their long program, splicing together four different pieces of music to make up their four and a half minutes. The wisdom of this was obvious: It is a way to show off your versatility and to advertise every strength.

Other forms of figure skating have had a similar three-step structure to their competitions, but that is where their similarity to ice dancing ends. Solo skating—such as the kind performed by Kristi Yamaguchi, Nancy Kerrigan, or Brian Boitano—has less emphasis on dance and more emphasis on feats of great athleticism and difficulty. A solo skater skates only a short program and a long program. The short one must include certain elements determined by the ISU, but the long one may include anything the skater wishes. Solo skating emphasizes spectacular moves—triple axels, sit-spins, salchows, and others and is less concerned with the steps in between those moves. In fact, the "steps in between" are often only a way for the skater to gain the speed and regain the stamina needed for his or her next big jump.

The same is true for pairs skating. Most pairs skaters also perform dazzling feats of derring-do—throws, lifts, spins, holds—but may do almost anything in between. Ice dancing, by contrast, is only concerned with what is "in between." It is the steps, the movement on the ice, and the interpretation of the music that most matter. All the acrobatics have been eliminated, making these programs about the skating, and nothing else.

As a young girl, Jayne studied both pairs and solo figure skating. At age twelve, she won the British junior pairs title with her partner, Michael Hutchinson. At thirteen, she and Michael placed second in the British Senior Pairs Championship. The next year, they won the British Pairs Championship—making them the best pairs figure skaters in all of Great Britain. This victory set them up to represent their country at the 1972 European Championships held in Gothenburg, Germany. Jayne and Michael's score earned them eighteenth place, which was not surprising given their ages and the short amount of time they had been on the seniors "circuit." Skaters usually have to spend many years in the ranks while the judges get to know them and their styles. Rarely do newcomers finish at the top.

Torvill and Hutchinson placed second at their next British Championship. At that point, Michael decided he wanted to move on: to a different trainer, to London, to a new partner if need be. Jayne, however, was not ready to leave Nottingham, and so, in 1973, she found herself working once again on her solo figure skating career, which she would continue to do until she hooked up with Christopher Dean two years later.

Christopher, unlike Jayne, had studied only ice dancing. When he first came to the rink to sign up for lessons, he chose ice dancing because his parents had done some ballroom dancing and they thought he might enjoy it. After two years of ice-dancing lessons, he found a partner, Sandra Elson, and together, they won the British Primary Dance Championship in 1972. Two years later, in 1974, they won the British Junior Dance Championship and placed sixth in the senior competition. But all was not well with Elson and Dean. Theirs was a tense relationship, full of explosions and arguments. In 1975, their coach, Len Sayward, who was employed by the Nottingham rink as coach and teacher to its patrons, left for another job. Sandra wanted to go with Sayward, but Chris, like Jayne, preferred to stay in Nottingham. Besides his reluctance to move, he also sensed that he and Sandra would not last as partners; their partnership was too volatile. Shortly after their coach departed, Sandra decided to leave Nottingham as well. Now Chris, like Jayne, was without a partner.

When Len Sayward left Nottingham, he was replaced by Janet Sawbridge, a three-time British ice-dancing champion who had also competed as a solo skater—an unusual combination. After she had been on the job only a few days, Sawbridge witnessed the tumultuous final practice and split of Elson and Dean. Now she had a serious problem to solve: Here was her promising student, Christopher Dean, at loose ends and in need of a partner. Sawbridge had noticed Jayne Torvill at the rink, and although Jayne was not an ice dancer, the coach knew that Jayne was also without a partner and looking to make a change in her skating. Sawbridge suggested that Jayne Torvill and Christopher Dean try skating together, just to see if they were a "good fit." The "fit" is important in ice dancing—if the man and woman are too different in height or proportion, the lines of their dancing will never be graceful, their arms will never have the proper extension, their legs will never be in perfect unison. In May 1975, Chris, Jayne, and Janet met to see if there was any possibility of them working as a team. Jayne is only 5-feet-^{1}/$_2$-inch tall, whereas Christopher is 5-feet-10-inches tall. Luckily, though, they looked just fine together, especially if Jayne extended her legs and arms as fully as possible. They agreed to meet for a practice session the next day.

That first practice session was fraught with tension for everyone. Jayne had ice danced only very rarely and could not remember most of the steps. Chris was desperate for a partner, and no one else was available. They were both painfully shy and worried about whether this partnership was a good idea. For Chris, the fear was that Jayne would not work out as a partner and that he would lose valuable time and competitive ground. For Jayne, the experiment was potentially humiliating—she had excelled in the pairs, but now she would be completely out of her element. The practice session did not go very well—there were no moments of discovery, no hint of "aha!" Jayne would later describe it as "ghastly." At one point, she fell and hit her elbow and her head. Some of the spectators at that practice thought they were a poor match for each other—and someone even told Chris as much, a comment they both would remember well in the years to come. Despite this lukewarm beginning, Janet Sawbridge liked what she saw: a confident young man and a determined young woman, trying to come together to dance as one.

Chris and Jayne decided to try to skate together for a month's trial period. After only a few weeks, they had improved so much that Janet Sawbridge asked some skating judges to watch them and give her an opinion. The judges were not overly wowed by Chris and Jayne's skating, but they were not negative about it either. Torvill and Dean took this as an encouraging sign.

In the autumn of 1975, just a few short months after the partners had come together, they entered a small competition in Bristol, England. Surprisingly, they came in second, ahead of many more-experienced couples and behind only the bronze medalists from the British Championships. This event, though relatively insignificant in the context of serious ice-dancing competition, was a turning point for Torvill and Dean. Their future now seemed bright: They were moving up in the ranks unusually fast, they worked together extremely well, they had practiced hard and made enormous progress in the four short months they had been together, and they competed well—something they would continue to do for the rest of their careers.

The pair now set their sights on bigger, more important competitions. But there were logistical

Jayne would later describe her first practice with Christopher as "ghastly."
❦ ❦ ❦ ❦ ❦

considerations and obstacles that made progress difficult to ensure. In 1975, Jayne turned eighteen, and Christopher turned seventeen. They were both working to support themselves and their skating. Jayne worked as a secretary at Norwich Union, an insurance company. Chris was a police cadet at the police academy. As children of rather modest means, they naturally assumed they would each have to work for a living. The skating was fun, and it was rewarding, but for now they never dreamt it could be a career. At some point, they assumed, their amateur skating days would come to an end.

This double commitment—to work and skating—would prove to be very demanding for both of them. In addition to their full-time jobs (or in Chris's case, full-time police training), they were skating anywhere from seventeen to twenty-one hours a week. They would take a lesson every evening for a half-hour, then practice for an additional hour-and-a-half during public skating hours. They would also have a two-hour session two mornings a week, plus a three-hour session every Sunday morning. This schedule left little time for socializing—or any other activities, for that matter. As a result, Chris and Jayne became very close friends.

In fact, there has been much speculation during their career about the nature of their partnership. Their ice dancing has always had a kind of emotional intensity, a romantic intimacy, that seemed impossible between two people who *were not* romantically involved. Over the years, they gave different answers to the inevitable questions about their relationship. Apparently, they were romantically involved early on in the partnership, but they eventually realized that they must invest all their emotions in their partnership *on* the ice, not off, and that any romantic intentions, impulses, plans, or desires had to wait until they had achieved their skating goals. This meant, however, that they were not involved with anyone else, either, and the intensity of their commitment to each other showed in their work.

It might be hard to understand how two teenagers could be so emotionally and physically disciplined for something that was, essentially, a hobby. This forms another clue to the dynamics of their partnership: They were both extremely dedicated people. Jayne was known for her grit. She would practice something over and over again until she got it right. If she stumbled on a step, she became all the more determined to perfect it the next time. If someone told her she could not do something, she would *do* it. Perhaps the skepticism that first greeted her pairing up with Chris is partially responsible for the later success of Torvill and Dean. It is just like Jayne to want to prove her detractors wrong and show that she could do anything she set her mind to. Christopher, too, was stubborn. His on-ice arguments with his former partner, Janet Elson, are testaments to that. He wanted things to be "just so" and would not rest—or let anyone else rest—until they were done to his liking. All who know Torvill and Dean agree that Jayne's ability to weather Chris's perfectionist storms with both her spirits and sense of humor intact was critical to their partnership.

Another clue to their unique determination might be their working-class backgrounds. However resigned they might have been to a life of office jobs and street beats, skating was a welcome diversion to a fairly predictable future. It provided an exciting and satisfying creative outlet, and, like any pursuit of excellence, it enriched their lives.

There was a certain synergy, too, to their early years: The harder they worked, the better they got. And they improved so quickly that it was all the more rewarding to work harder still. It would be impossible to say exactly why they came so far so fast, but there are some factors that, in retrospect, seem important. First of all, Jayne's figure-skating background made her a very able skater. She had great technique on the ice. As Chris would say about her in later years, "It's Jayne who makes it possible. She can do anything I ask her to." This made her an ideal partner for Chris, who has long been considered the more creative half of the partnership. It is he who always choreographed their routines, who always imagined the new steps, who devised the new ways to put blade on ice to music.

In the final analysis, it was hard work and persistence that made Torvill and Dean everything they would become. As 1984 Olympic men's solo figure-skating champion Scott Hamilton of the United States put it: "No one works harder than Torvill and Dean. Not me. Not anyone."

Chapter 2

Honing the Competitive Edge

Their early years together were spent

putting in long hours perfecting steps,

working on every detail, every nuance of

their performances.

By the winter of 1975–1976, Chris and Jayne were preparing for their first competitive season. This meant long hours at the rink and a number of hurdles to be overcome. Luckily, Chris's parents had recently moved just a few blocks from Jayne's, which put him nearer the rink. This move cut down on his commuting time, giving the partners a few more precious minutes on the ice every week.

But there were competitive as well as logistical challenges to be met that winter, one of which was the "Inter-gold" test. This test would enable them to compete in the British Championships later that year. For the test, a couple performs a dance twice; the first time, the man is judged; the second time, the woman is judged. During their first pass at the rumba—while Chris was being judged—they made an error in the timing, and Chris did not pass. Their coach, Janet Sawbridge, recognized the problem and gave them some quick coaching in between the two performances. Poor Chris had to put his own disappointment aside and skate his very best for Jayne's turn. And he did. Jayne passed. They would eventually re-skate the Inter-gold, and both would pass in plenty of time for their upcoming competitions. This episode was telling of the partners. When the stakes were high, they were able to pull through, not only for the sake of the program but for each other. They did not become discouraged, but rather were challenged by failure and difficulty. This quality would stand them in good stead in the years to come.

Under Janet Sawbridge's guidance and coaching, Torvill and Dean began entering, and sometimes winning, more competitions. Their first victory came at a small competition in Sheffield, England. Their first title came in April 1976, at the Northern Championships held in Bristol, England.

Shortly afterwards, the National Skating Association (NSA) of Britain chose Jayne and Chris to travel to two esteemed international competitions. The speed with which they were recognized by the NSA was unusual—they had been together only a year. The first competition was at Oberstdorf, Germany.

For Chris and Jayne, the competition was a challenge to both their skating prowess and their budgets. First of all, they had to arrange to take the time off from their jobs, and, while the NSA would pay half of their expenses, the money would only come after the competition, not before. As a result, the secretary and the police cadet had to keep an extremely tight budget. (This meant eating rarely and cheaply and even brewing coffee on the sly in their hotel room!) Because Janet was not able to accompany them, they also had to practice on their own and coach themselves to improvement.

They came in second at Oberstdorf, beaten by a Soviet couple. The Soviets had long dominated ice dancing and would continue to be Torvill and Dean's main competition.

Their next international competition, in the summer of 1976, was in St. Gervais, France. This time, the Soviets were not competing, and Torvill and Dean won the competition. Now, they were "on the map," judges would start to take notice, and the skating world surely would begin to recognize their names.

Next, they skated in their first British Championships, which was held in their hometown of Nottingham in the fall of 1976. They came in fourth, earning themselves a place as the reserve ice dancers on the British team to the European and World championships. As it turned out, they were not called upon to go, but being the reserves was another success that gave them a real vote of confidence.

The winter after the British Championships—1976–1977—was their introduction to the endless hard work required, day after day, year after year, to move up in the ice-dancing world. Now would come a real test of their commitment. Could they keep it up for the long haul? This would be a daunting question for any ice-dancing couple, but it became even harder to answer given their particular circumstances.

As part of his police-cadet training, Chris was sent for ten weeks to Dishforth, a town about two hours away from Nottingham by car. Commuting daily was impossible, so Chris and Jayne had only the weekends to practice. It was an exhausting ordeal for Chris, who trained all week and skated furiously all weekend. For Jayne, it was frustrating to wait impatiently throughout the week, or to practice by herself, and then try to bolster up her bone-tired partner for the two precious days they had together each week. Chris claims that several times he advised Jayne to find another partner so that she would not have to put up with his difficult schedule. But Jayne persisted. She never gave up on him or their partnership.

After Dishforth, she would have ample opportunity to show her commitment, as the logistics of his training and job continued to make their lives miserable. Christopher was next sent for more training to Epperstone, which was a 45-minute drive away. Their schedule for those five weeks was grueling: Jayne would wake up, drive to Epperstone, pick up Chris, drive them both back to the Nottingham rink for a 6:00 a.m. rehearsal, and then he would drive back to Epperstone. They would both put in a full day's work, then Chris would drive back to Nottingham for several more hours of practice in the evening before Jayne drove him home and got a few hours of sleep before the ordeal began again.

But their perseverance over the winter paid off. In the summer of 1977 they returned to the competition in Oberstdorf, where they had placed second the year before. This time they won. Now they had two international titles to their name! The titles were not the biggest or most prestigious in skating, but they boosted the pair's confidence nonetheless.

For Torvill and Dean, the competitive season usually ran from the fall through the winter: smaller competitions came first, then the British Championships in November, followed by (if

they qualified) the European Championships in
January, the Olympics (if it was an Olympic year)
in February, and the World Championships in
March. Skaters prepare their various programs
over the spring and summer. They know what
the compulsories will be and what kind of music
they will need to use for the short program.
And, of course, they must decide on and design
their long program. Once the skaters' programs
are set, they compete all season with the same
material. Too much work goes into each element
to prepare something new for each competition.
Judges also like to see the same program over
the course of a season to become familiar with it
so that they can judge it carefully.

The British Championships awaited in November of 1977. The year before, they had
placed fourth. Their hope was not to win it—it
is virtually unheard of to skip from fourth to first
place in one year—but to keep moving up, one
place at a time. And they did. They came in
third, becoming the British bronze medalists for
the first time. In addition to the thrill of getting
a medal, third place also won them a spot on the
European and World teams. Chris and Jayne
would, at last, be sharing the ice with the most
accomplished skaters in the world.

In January 1978, Chris and Jayne headed to
Strasbourg, France, for their first European
Championship competition. It was a struggle for
them—they had to raise the money to pay for

By 1977, Chris and Jayne were allowed to share the ice with the most accomplished skaters in the world.

their coach, Janet Sawbridge, to come with them. Also, Janet had recently found out she was pregnant and, they feared, might be losing interest in coaching. They were painfully shy at this point in their lives, too, and that made large competitions doubly intimidating. At the same time, of course, they were also very excited to be there and to see for themselves the ice dancers they had idolized on television. As eager pupils, they tried to soak up as much wisdom and information as possible from everyone they watched.

Andrei Minenkov and Irina Moiseyeva from the (then) USSR were the reigning ice dancers of that era. Torvill and Dean were especially impressed by their expressiveness on the ice. They also took note of the precompetition rituals of Krisztina Regoeczy and Andras Sallay of Hungary—especially their relaxed and affectionate manner. Chris and Jayne were "looked after" by Warren Maxwell and Janet Thompson, the current British ice-dancing champions, which was also extremely helpful.

The pair from Nottingham also learned a great deal about their own skating at the competition. A particular compulsory, called the Starlight waltz, would teach them much about their abilities. They skated it eighteenth out of nineteen couples. The ice was very choppy and cut up from all the couples who had skated before them. Working against this difficult surface, they could both feel that they did not have the proper stamina, that their haphazard, part-time training schedule had not prepared them adequately.

Nevertheless, they forged ahead and came in ninth. Breaking the "top ten" was another important success. They were also pleased because having another couple in the top ten would enable the British team to enter more skaters in the next season's competition. The European Championship was an important step in Torvill and Dean's hike to the top—they had been seen by their fellow Britons on television, they had met the best teams in the sport, and they had made a good showing in their first high-profile international competition.

Now it was time to concentrate on the World Championships in Ottawa, Canada, in March 1978. After the high of Strasbourg, they had to head straight back home to their work, their practice schedules, and their skating routines. Janet Sawbridge was becoming less and less accessible—in fact, she gave them only one lesson in the weeks between the Europeans and the Worlds! Because of her pregnancy, she would not be able to accompany her students to Ottawa, either. Chris and Jayne virtually had to coach themselves, adding even more pressure to their already overloaded lives.

Ottawa, like Strasbourg, was a thrill, but a bit of a disappointment, too. They came in eleventh, lower than they had hoped. They felt that they were not as well-conditioned physically as they should be, that their odd hours and no-sleep training schedule were not keeping them in competitive condition. Another negative was that Ottawa made them very aware of their lack of coaching. Janet Sawbridge's slow fade from their lives was beginning to take its toll. The positive aspect of Ottawa was exposure: Seeing all the other couples gave them lots of new ideas and great inspiration for the season to come.

When they returned to Nottingham, Janet Sawbridge was in the hospital with her new baby. Chris and Jayne were not at all surprised to hear that she wanted to retire from coaching. In fact, they were relieved. In order to keep making progress, they needed more attention than they had been getting from Janet, who, with a new baby, would have even less time for them.

Now all they needed to do was find a new coach, and it would have to be someone local, because Chris was still committed to his police job. They approached Roy Sanders, the manager of the Nottingham ice stadium, for advice. Sanders put in a call to Betty Callaway, a well-known ice-dancing coach. Oddly, Callaway had never been a competitive ice dancer, but she had performed in ice shows in her youth and had trained to be a skating teacher. She was known for her expertise in the compulsory dances. She was British but had never coached a British couple. Her current protégés were

Krisztina Regoeczy and Andras Sallay, the Hungarian couple Chris and Jayne had admired at the Europeans just a few months before.

When Roy Sanders called Betty Callaway, she had just received a letter from her Hungarian couple. After reading the letter, it seemed to Betty that they had decided to retire, freeing her up to take on a new pair. She was vaguely aware of Torvill and Dean—she had seen them at the Europeans and Worlds and had even commented to Regoeczy and Sallay: "I like our new British couple." At the Worlds, she had shared an elevator with Chris and had handed a costume to Jayne in the dressing room. Her main impression was that they were terribly shy—which they were—and that they had potential.

Betty Callaway told Roy Sanders she would be willing to meet with Torvill and Dean, and would make her decision then. For her, the most important thing would be to genuinely like the couple. A coach spends too much time with her "kids" for personality conflicts. Luckily, when they met at the ice rink, Betty liked Jayne and Chris very much, and they all agreed to enter into a coaching relationship. Between their jobs and various grants from the NSA, the Nottingham City Council, and the Sports Aid Foundation, Chris and Jayne managed to find the money to pay Betty's coaching fees.

Right after the three of them became a team, Betty Callaway heard from Regoeczy and Sallay.

Apparently they had not retired, and they had never intended to; Betty had simply misunderstood their letter. She felt committed to Regoeczy and Sallay—but also now to Chris and Jayne. Betty would honor both obligations, and, as it would turn out, this arrangement would be beneficial to everyone.

Together, the couples and their coach came up with a solution. During the week, Betty would work with her Hungarian students in London, and on the weekends, the three of them would travel to Nottingham to train with Chris and Jayne. At the end of the weekend, Betty would give Chris and Jayne things to work on together during the next week.

The arrangement worked well. Regoeczy and Sallay had maturity and flair on the ice—exactly what Chris and Jayne lacked and needed to acquire. By training with and observing the Hungarians, Torvill and Dean were reaping the benefits of Regoeczy and Sallay's ballet training and were picking up some of their sophistication. The shared training helped Regoeczy and Sallay, too. Chris and Jayne were already so technically excellent that Betty used them to demonstrate technique and placement to the Hungarians. Betty's coaching style was very relaxed, supportive, and educational. She never berated her skaters, never tried to bully them into doing something the right way. Rather, she saw her job as teaching her skaters to think for themselves. When a step was wrong, Betty would stop the couple and ask them what they thought was wrong and why. In this way, her skaters could improve on their own by thinking through the moves and being able to make educated decisions.

Since Betty's coaching strength was in the compulsories, she coached those dances more closely. On the short and free programs, Betty saw herself more as a sounding board, an educated and interested audience. This made her an ideal coach for Torvill and Dean. Already strong in technique but hungry to be ever better, they lapped up the precision coaching Betty offered for the compulsories. But, with Christopher's burgeoning flair for choreography, it worked well that Betty first gave him room to create without criticism, before stepping in later to help finesse the details.

Chris and Jayne worked conscientiously during the week, but, as before, they did so under grueling conditions. Christopher was now a police officer, working different shifts—sometimes 8 a.m. to 4 p.m., sometimes 2 p.m. to 10 p.m., sometimes 5 p.m. to 1 a.m. Jayne was still working during the day. Luckily, she had "flex time" at work, which allowed her some latitude in her hours, but Chris's schedule often meant they spent late hours at the rink, sometimes with no sleep at all before Jayne's next day at work. An officemate of Jayne's later said that "she was

An officemate of Jayne's later said that "she was always very tired. Sometimes we would find her slumped over her typewriter!"

❦❦❦❦❦

always very tired. Sometimes we would find her slumped over her typewriter!" But Chris and Jayne never tired of it. They always looked forward to more practice, more hard work, and, ultimately, more fun.

Their commitment and the new coaching arrangement soon began to pay off. Shortly after Betty joined them, in the summer of 1978, they won Britain's John Davis Trophy. In November 1978, they entered their third British Championship and received their first 6.0—a perfect score—from one of the judges. They also scored a 5.8 and a 5.9 from a British judge who had never given out a 6.0. Only three-and-a-half years after coming together, and just a few months after teaming up with Betty Callaway, Torvill and Dean had won a gold medal at the British Championships!

Chris and Jayne were now also maturing as skaters. They had jumped from third place to first place in the British Championships. They were training with a world-class coach. They were friends and training partners with one of the best ice-dancing couples in the world and they were heading for their second European and World championships. In the time between the British Championships and the Europeans, Torvill and Dean traveled to Regoeczy and Sallay's home in Budapest, Hungary. This would prove to be an important trip. There, they studied with Zoltan Nagy, a well-known Hungarian ballet dancer. Nagy had a particular impact on Chris, showing him how balletic grace can be strong and powerful, beautiful and easy. Nagy's ballet influence improved their posture, their physical attitudes, and their choreography.

Jayne and Chris were also beginning to develop competitive strategies and superstitious rituals—another sign that they were "making it" in amateur skating. For example, they always laced up their left skate first. Before they stepped out onto the ice, they lined up their skate guards in a precise row of four and placed them right next to the rink. Chris always stepped out onto the ice with his left foot first. Jayne wore the same pair of ice-skate earrings for every competition. (As ridiculous as these rituals may sound, they are not at all unusual among world-class athletes.)

After Budapest, it was time for the 1979 European Championships at Zagreb, Yugoslavia (now in Croatia). Just as they had hoped, they moved up in the ranks: This time they placed sixth, three spaces up from the previous year's ninth-place finish. In March 1979, they competed in their second World Championships in Vienna. They came in eighth, also three places up from 1978's eleventh place showing. More importantly, their scores were getting steadily better. The judges liked what they were seeing, and that could only bode well for the future. Vienna made them happy for another reason:

Regoeczy and Sallay were the silver medalists, placing second in the world.

At this point, the routine was familiar: After the World Championships, it was time to work up a new set of dances for the next season. Chris and Jayne set about it with their usual enthusiasm and crazy hours. During that summer of 1979, however, they had an unique opportunity: A colleague of Betty Callaway's had rented a rink in Switzerland for two weeks and asked if she would like to come and visit with her couples. Chris and Jayne scraped together enough vacation time from their jobs and went. It was the first time they had ever had nearly unlimited time on the ice. They could practice as much as they wanted, for as long as they wanted, and at civilized times of the day! To them, it was a revelation, a glimpse of what training could be, if they only had the luxury of unlimited money and time! Zoltan Nagy joined them there, and they were able to put in long hours perfecting steps, working on every detail, every nuance of their performances.

They began the 1979–1980 season with two international competitions. In the Rotary Watches competition (later known as the St. Ivel) in Richmond, England, they came in second. Perhaps more significantly, they beat Regoeczy and Sallay's scores on the free dance. At the NHK Trophy competition in Tokyo, Japan, they also came in second. This time, their high scores gave notice to their Soviet idols, Moiseyeva and Minenkov. In November 1979, they won the British Championship for the second time in a row. As a result, they were invited to a reception at Number 10 Downing Street, home of then British Prime Minister, Margaret Thatcher. Jayne managed to sneak a peek at the bathroom. "Can you imagine who must have used this place!?" she said to Chris later.

Winning the British gold meant that they would head to the Europeans and the Worlds for

Chris and Jayne practice their routine at the St. Ivel rink in Richmond, England.

the third time. Because it was 1980, they would also make their first trip to the Olympics, in Lake Placid, New York. This meant, of course, more time off from their jobs, more training, and more traveling. But it was worth it.

At the Europeans in Gothenburg, Germany, Chris came down with the stomach flu. He survived on black tea and crackers, still managing, somehow, to skate well. Torvill and Dean ended up in fourth place.

Their experience at Lake Placid caused them to feel a mixture of impatience and frustration, excitement, disappointment, and pride. The impatience and frustration had to do with the Olympics themselves: The skaters were housed in a former prison, transportation to and from the sporting arenas and ceremonial events was disastrously slow and inadequate, and the daily security precautions and logistical requirements were exhausting. Of course, they were excited to be part of the Olympics at all—it is the "ultimate" event for any athlete. Their fifth-place finish was a disappointment, but they took solace in the fact that their scores were getting higher each time they competed. They were proud of their fellow countryman, Robin Cousins, the classy Briton who won the gold medal in the men's solo skating event. After the Olympics, they still had to gear up for the 1980 World Championships in Dortmund, Germany, where they came in a respectable fourth.

After Dortmund, the cycle began again. But could they keep it up? How much farther could they climb in ice dancing? And could they achieve the highest level while training every night from 10:30 p.m. on and then rousing themselves for another day at the office, another stroll on the beat? The two weeks in Switzerland had been a tantalizing hint of how much they could accomplish if they could devote themselves to skating full-time. But how would they be able to afford it? And if they were able to support themselves while training full-time, would it be a worthwhile gamble? Would they later regret giving up good jobs that would have seen them to their retirement years?

The answers would come with another invitation in the summer of 1980, this time from Oberstdorf, site of some of Torvill and Dean's early international competitions. Betty said that she would come and help train some German skaters, but only if her students could come, too. The Germans agreed, and Betty was able to secure five weeks of training at Oberstdorf for Chris and Jayne. The facilities there were a world apart from their home rink in Nottingham. Several rinks were available exclusively for training, some with mirrors running the length of the rink so the skaters could watch their every move. There were rehearsal studios, other athletic facilities, and lodging. Chris and Jayne would be able to immerse themselves in skating full-time, instead of grabbing an hour here or there when the Nottingham rink was closed to the public.

They "cashed in" all the vacation time, paid and unpaid leave, and good will that they could get from their employers and took five weeks off. Their time at Oberstdorf was a welcome opportunity. It was a relief for them to be thinking only of skating. And it was wonderful to develop routines in front of the mirror, to see what they were doing right or wrong for themselves. After five weeks of intense training and steady improvement, they knew there was no turning back. If they were to achieve all that they hoped they could, they would need to quit their jobs and train full-time.

This was not a casual decision. They had no obvious sources of money, and they would need money to pay for coaching, rink time, and living expenses. Nevertheless, they both gave notice at their jobs. For Chris, the decision to leave the force was an emotional one. He had been imagining a future as a police officer for a long time. He had trained hard and worked hard. His employers were equally attached to Chris. His boss offered him an unpaid leave, more flexibility, whatever it would take to keep Chris on the force. But Chris was firm—he finally knew where his heart was, and it was not on the beat. Chris's boss agreed to let him go only five days after Chris had returned from Oberstdorf.

Unfortunately, Jayne was not able to leave her job as quickly. Although she was less attached to her line of work than Chris was to his, she had more days to "make up" for all the time she had been away. For three weeks Jayne had to stick with her job, knowing that Chris was already free of his other obligations, knowing that her future awaited.

The day finally came when Chris and Jayne were both "free," both ready to skate all day, every day. But, there was still the pressing problem of money.

Their first stroke of luck was receiving a grant from the Sports Aid Foundation for £8,000 (more than $15,000) to be used over the next three-and-a-half years—until the 1984 Olympics in Sarajevo, Yugoslavia. The money was welcome, but it would not be enough to get them to Sarajevo. It did, however, allow them to train for, and begin, the 1980–1981 season. They returned to Richmond for the St. Ivel competition and won it. In November 1980 came their fifth British Championship competition, which they won again for the third time.

One day, after the British but before the European championships, a member of the Nottingham City Council stopped by Jayne's parents' news shop and mentioned that a request for training funds to the City Council might be worth a shot. Jayne and Chris quickly calculated the minimum that they would need to train in

Queen Elizabeth offers her encouragement to Chris and Jayne after they won their third British Championship in a row.

Nottingham for the next three World Championships and the 1984 Olympics: £14,000 a year for the next three years. They submitted the proposal and waited.

They heard it on the radio first. The City Council would give them the full amount: £42,000 over the next three years. Unfortunately, there was some criticism in the press. Some taxpayers felt it was the wrong use of public money. Chris and Jayne agreed to publicize Nottingham as much as possible—wearing the city name on their jackets, etc.—but this did not appease everyone. The skaters felt badly about the criticism, but were also relieved.

With this enormous life decision made, and with adequate funds at last, Torvill and Dean prepared for the European Championships. Between November and February, they worked extremely hard on their program, training both in Nottingham and in Oberstdorf, where they could get more time on the ice. Although they had won the British Championships, the Europeans would be far more competitive, and they wanted to show the city of Nottingham that its faith—and its money—had not been misplaced. They had been moving up steadily every year and felt that this year they might get a medal at Europeans or Worlds, which would be a nice reflection on their city, their country, and, of course, on them.

They were required to use a cha-cha for their short program that year, a Latin-American dance with a tricky rhythm and distinctive arm and hip movements. Because they felt that their cha-cha at the British had not been authentic enough, they decided to consult a Latin dance expert, who taught them in his dance studio and went to the rink with them to translate the dance onto the ice. This attention to detail was typical of Torvill and Dean's quest for perfection. They used whatever resources they could find to "get it exactly right." They kept working on a routine even after the season had begun. Every nuance, and every performance, mattered to them—and it showed.

44

Their long program, or free dance, that year was a traditional four-part collage of music and dance styles. They danced jazz to a selection from "Fame," an Egyptian-style section to "Caravan," a rumba to "Red Sails in the Sunset," and swing to Benny Goodman's "Swing, Swing, Swing." After the Worlds, they set out for Innsbruck, Austria, in January 1981, full of high hopes and great expectations. Now was the time to make their move.

On Top of the World–and Beyond

"They were technically brilliant…The

timing was flawless…They've got a magic

personality on the ice."

—*Pamela Davis, Skating Judge*

Torvill and Dean arrived at Innsbruck with one objective: to face the top couples in the world and maybe nudge one or two of them aside to capture a bronze or silver medal. Their chief competition was three Soviet couples. Andrei Minenkov and Irina Moiseyeva (dubbed "Min and Mo" by the British press) and Natalya Linichuk and Gennadi Karponosov (winners of the 1980 Winter Olympics) were established stars from the country that had dominated ice dance for the past twelve years.

45

Also present was the up-and-coming Natalia Bestemianova and Andrei Bukin (nicknamed "B and B" by the British press). Min and Mo had long been idols of Chris and Jayne, but now that Torvill and Dean were finally poised to break into the top three, they would be skating directly against these pros. It was intimidating company.

As usual, Chris and Jayne stayed away from the press, not wanting to make predictions or answer too many questions. Some of this behavior can be attributed to their shyness, but some of it came from a deliberate decision not to be distracted from the skating by *anything*. They would need that concentration, too, because the practice facilities at Innsbruck were dreadful. Freezing cold, with water dripping through the ceiling, the practice rink was a former speed-skating rink that had been "converted" for figure skating through the use of wooden barricades that defined a smaller oval in the middle. Practice sessions at big competitions serve a number of purposes. Of course, the skaters need to go through their routines to stay in mental and physical shape, but they also need to practice in front of an audience and in front of the judges. Having an audience helps the skaters gauge the kind of reaction they might get at their final performance. Letting the judges see the program ahead of time helps them score more carefully at the actual competitive performance. Because the judges are already familiar with the distinct elements and the difficulty level of the program, they can focus on the *execution* of the routine instead. Unfortunately, the practice rink at Innsbruck was so cold and off-putting that no one came to watch. This situation was disconcerting for all the skaters— especially for "newcomers" Torvill and Dean.

In some small way, however, having miserable practice facilities may have helped. Maybe the judges, having less exposure to the routines and skaters ahead of time, kept their minds and eyes open to the couples who were on their way up. In any case, after the first compulsory, a Westminster waltz, Chris and Jayne found themselves in an unlikely place: first. Later, Jayne remembered her feelings at the time: "We felt quite depressed whenever we had to use that [practice] rink. The main rink was nice and we quite enjoyed the competition of course! We did the first dance, the Westminster waltz, really well. By that time we had had so many minor irritations, and some not so minor, that we weren't really thinking about which place we would get, only about getting through the thing with our sanity intact."

Their next compulsory was a *paso doble*—a quick Latin dance that comes from the bullfighting tradition. This time around, they felt more self-conscious about their skating because they were now in the lead. Again they won, and, all of a sudden, they were the front runners! As they left the stadium, they found themselves facing a crush of microphones and reporters' questions about how it felt to be in the lead. They were unprepared for such interest so early in the competition and didn't feel at all smug about their current number-one status. They knew all too well that the bulk of the competition was yet to come and that they could very easily lose their lead to their Soviet competitors, whose specialty was the more-expressive free dance program.

Chris and Jayne still had one more compulsory (a rumba) to go, plus their short program (the cha-cha they had worked so hard to improve after the British Championships), and the free dance. After a night's sleep, they returned to the rink and aced the rumba, winning again. Now it was time for the cha-cha short program. Unfortunately, they were due to skate it second out of nineteen couples. Just as skaters do not like to skate late in a competition, when the ice is full of ruts from the previous participants, they also do not like to skate early, especially if they are medal contenders. They prefer a later placement because they feel that the judges often "save" the higher scores for the end. A judge does not want to run the risk of giving an early couple a very high score, only to see a later couple do a much better job and not have "room" to give the later couple adequately high points. If you have given out a 6.0 and somebody later skates better than that, what can you do? With their early placement in the field, Chris and Jayne fully expected to drop back in the rankings. But, once again, their hard work and new, improved training schedule paid off: Six judges placed them first; the other three put them second behind only Min and Mo. Miraculously, they were still in the lead with only the free dance to go.

This time they had better luck in their placement: They would be skating *after* their main competition, Min and Mo. They purposely did not allow themselves to hear Min and Mo's scores before they took to the ice. They needed to concentrate on the skating—nothing else. They skated to the center of the rink and waited for their music to start. "This is the worst time of all," said Jayne later. "It may seem not much more than the blink of an eye but time seems to stand still as you wait and wonder if something might go wrong." But nothing did go wrong.

Later, neither of them would remember much of what happened on the ice for those four minutes in Innsbruck, Austria, in January 1981. They performed as well as they ever had— no mistakes, no moments of doubt, no worries from start to finish. They were on a high— skating their very best, regardless of the results. The results, though would bring another high to the Nottingham couple: They were placed

"It may seem not much more than the blink of an eye but time seems to stand still as you wait and wonder if something might go wrong."

first by eight out of the nine judges. Torvill and Dean had won their first European Championship! A flood of emotions—exhilaration, disbelief, relief—swept over both of them simultaneously.

That high, however, would not last for long. When they returned to England, they were greeted with accolades, but also with more criticism about the Nottingham City Council grant they had received. Some people felt that if they were to receive British funds, specifically Nottingham funds, they should do all their training in Nottingham—not in Oberstdorf, Germany. There was some grumbling about how much more expensive it must have been to train in another country at such high-level facilities. Chris and Jayne, however, had not spent a penny more than they had estimated they would spend—and they had based their estimate on training in Nottingham. They had always intended to train at home but they could not get enough time on the ice. The Nottingham rink was a public facility, open most of the day to anyone who wished to skate.

Chris and Jayne chose not to answer all their critics. They came to understand that once they were in the public eye, their every action would be scrutinized and judged and they would never be able to please everyone. In their hearts, they knew they had done the right thing with their grant money.

The second thing that brought them back down to earth after Innsbruck was the upcoming World Championships in March 1981, to be held in Hartford, Connecticut. Torvill and Dean were in the unusual position of being the favored couple, but they had been competing long enough to know they were not a shoo-in for the title. After all, the European Championships had not included the very strong skaters from North America, and their presence would change the dynamics of the competition a great deal. Besides, anything could happen: an injury, a slip on rutted ice, even just a bad day could make the crucial tenth-of-a-point difference between medals. That's why concentration and focus would be critical.

In fact, injury was a factor soon enough. Evidently, Chris had been feeling some pain in one leg during practice sessions at Innsbruck. He had stayed quiet about it so as not to alarm Jayne or alert the press, but now that he was back in England, he consulted a doctor, who found that Chris had a stress fracture. The couple continued to train at home and in Oberstdorf, but they had to be careful of Chris's leg and were prepared to leave the ice at any sign of a strain.

When they arrived in Hartford for the Worlds, they continued to be cautious. When a reporter asked them about Innsbruck, Chris answered, "Innsbruck? What happened there?"

It seemed Torvill and Dean would take nothing for granted—they had to view each competition as a completely separate event, to be won on its own terms.

Their main competition would once again be Min and Mo and B and B, plus the Americans Judy Blumberg and Michael Seibert. The *paso doble* compulsory came first, considered by Chris and Jayne to be their weakest routine. They outscored everybody, however, and were once again leaders in the competition. Next came the rumba, which Torvill and Dean felt was their strong suit. Surprisingly, their scores were not much higher than Min and Mo's, although one judge gave them a 5.9—a score that is almost never seen in the compulsories. They had the highest scores for the Westminster waltz—the next compulsory—and also won the cha-cha short program.

Now there was only the free program to skate. Even though Chris and Jayne had been the high scorers in the compulsories and short program, the differences in the total points were very small, and the free dance counted for a full 50 percent of the final score. Torvill and Dean were by no means finished with this competition.

Chris and Jayne purposely stayed quiet and aloof while they awaited their time on the ice. They never wanted to know how the other couples were doing or to be distracted by conversation or other worries. Of the final set of four couples, Chris and Jayne were slated to skate first. While it was a relief to "get it over with" early, they were worried that their scores might be lower because the judges would want to leave room for the possible better programs of later couples.

They stepped out onto the ice. Chris started skating around and suddenly left the rink. Jayne panicked. Could it be his leg? Had it finally given out? No. He had merely stepped out onto the ice with the "wrong" foot—his right instead of his left—and wanted to leave the ice and do it over. After correcting his mistake, Chris joined Jayne in the center of the rink. They skated their free program even better than they had at Innsbruck, receiving a total of nine 5.9s and nine 5.8s, at a time when 6.0s were virtually unheard of.

Then, it was backstage to wait. Jayne took a walk. Chris sat very still in the dressing room. At one point, he remembers hearing a gasp from the audience—Blumberg and Seibert had fallen. He did not know how anyone had scored. Jayne returned from her walk. Again, they waited. Finally, Betty Callaway, their coach, walked in and said, "Well, we've done it." The kids from Nottingham, the former bobby and secretary, were, suddenly, the best ice dancers in the world: They had actually won the World Champion-ships of 1981!

After the thrill wore off, both skaters felt utterly drained. Only now could they see how much pressure they had felt coming into the World and European championships. Only now could they feel how much they had wanted it. And only now could they appreciate how hard they had worked.

Each year, after the World Championships, the International Skating Union sponsors a tour of the championships' skaters. This time, Torvill and Dean would be featured players in that tour. As soon as they could pack, they were off for a grueling month of exhibitions around North America. Only after that tour was over could they return to Nottingham and appreciate how proud everyone in England was of them. This time, there was no criticism about their grant or their training location. Instead, there were piles of mail, a warm civic reception, and appearances on radio and television.

Chris and Jayne's total commitment to skating was obvious in the wake of their triumphant World Championship. During that time, they barely took a day off to rest. Knowing that they would have to outdo themselves to stay on top of the Worlds for 1982 and 1983, and then go for the Olympic gold in 1984, they could not waste any time between seasons. Though they performed almost every day during the tour, they returned to Nottingham and set to work on the next season's program.

Ice dancers are always looking for good music. Unlike other forms of skating, where the music seems incidental to the jumps and spins, ice dancing is wholly dependent on the music. The compulsories are *defined* by the music used, and the short and free programs also are judged by how well the skating *expresses* the music. Chris and Jayne would often go to a local Nottingham radio station to listen to selections from its vast library of recordings. Several years earlier, they had pulled out a recording of an ill-fated Broadway musical called *Mack and Mabel*. It was the story of the tumultuous relationship between silent-film director Mack Sennett and his leading lady, Mabel Normand, and it lasted nine days on Broadway. Torvill and Dean gave the Jerry Herman score a listen anyway and liked what they heard.

Chris had been toying with a new idea for their free program. He was trying to think of fresh approaches to their skating, unexpected ways of attacking the short and long programs. *Mack and Mabel* fit right into this new idea. Long programs, as mentioned, had traditionally consisted of four distinct pieces of music that showed off four separate ice-dancing styles. But what if an ice-dancing program was approached in the same way as a dance performance: as one integrated program that tells a story, progressing smoothly from section to section, from beginning to end?

As Chris's idea took root, he shared it with Jayne and Betty. Both were skeptical. Would it be considered legal? Would they be penalized because it was so different? Would they be able to show off their versatility well enough with a single musical piece? Jayne loved the music but fought to include a rumba somewhere in the middle because that dance showed them off to their best advantage.

Without deciding exactly where they would go with it, Chris and Jayne began to experiment with possible routines for the *Mack and Mabel* music. Having no specific dance form in mind, they let the music inspire them to find moves that would express the romantic spirit of the piece exactly. They also wanted to include some of the melodrama of Mack and Mabel's relationship and to give a "silent movie" feel to their free dance.

The duo spent hours in front of the mirrors at Oberstdorf, struggling to find just the right moves. Christopher sometimes lost his temper, impatient with himself for not being able to get everything right at once. Jayne stayed calm and coaxed Chris into trying again and again. Betty watched and reacted—and if she felt they had stopped being productive and needed a break, she insisted that they leave the ice. This monitoring was necessary because Chris and Jayne would work themselves ragged over the tiniest detail if left to their own devices. And whatever

quibbles erupted on the ice, Betty insisted that
they be left there.

Gradually, Jayne and Betty were won over
to Christopher's vision of a "Mack and Mabel"
program as one integrated piece. They, too,
began to appreciate the seamlessness of it, the
pleasure of its consistency. Inspired, they forged
on together to bring it to life.

As "Mack and Mabel" took shape, Chris and
Jayne had to work up a short program as well.
The required musical style for the 1981–1982
season's short program was the blues. They
settled on a harmonica version of George
Gershwin's "Summertime" from the opera *Porgy
and Bess.* As played by Larry Adler, the piece was
at the slowest tempo allowed by the International Skating Union. Once again, it was
important to Chris and Jayne that they take the
opportunity do something different, to push
themselves and the boundaries of what was
allowed in ice dancing. This very slow, very
moody version of "Summertime" would cer-
tainly stand out and do the trick.

One day, they spent two hours getting the
knee movements on one step exactly right. They
spent an hour or more another night on the
finishing pose alone. Jayne kept falling down as
they tried to get some move or other perfected.
"With some of the stuff we do," Jayne remarked
later, "you can look like raw beginners until you
get it right."

They returned to Nottingham from Oberstdorf at the end of the summer, 1981. They now had their programs choreographed and had only to polish them. First, though, they felt they needed to run their routines past some skating judges to make sure the slow "Summertime" and the unified "Mack and Mabel" would pass muster. They asked two judges from Birmingham to come to Nottingham. The results were better than they had hoped. One of the judges was jumping up and down with excitement. They both advised the skaters not to change a thing—both programs were perfect.

In September, they returned to Richmond, England, for the St. Ivel competition. "Summertime" was a hit, earning them one perfect 6.0. "Mack and Mabel," in particular, was a sensation. Jayne had so much fun skating it, she was surprised when it was over. It won them another three 6.0s.

Shortly after the St. Ivel, Chris and Jayne were honored with M.B.E.s (for member of the "Order of the British Empire") by the Queen of England—a huge honor for any Briton. Jayne— ever aware of their tight budget—was annoyed to find that while she had to buy an expensive outfit (complete with hat) to wear, Christopher could rent his morning suit and top hat. In fact, when the rental shop realized who he was and why he was renting the suit, they let him have it for free!

Chris and Jayne pose proudly with their M.B.E.s, awarded to them at Buckingham Palace in October 1981.

They spent the night before at a friend's house in London. The official ceremony was not too long or elaborate, but they were impressed to find that the Queen knew just who they were and all about their skating. She told them she was glad they had brought the world ice-dancing title back to Britain after twelve years. Even though it was a great honor and a thrill for Torvill and Dean, by 11 o'clock that night they were both back on the ice preparing for the British Championships coming up the next month.

The British Championships of 1981 were particularly intense. Because there were so few skaters entered that year, the entire competition was held in a day. This change meant that Chris and Jayne would perform three compulsories and their short and long programs all in the space of a few hours. By the time they made it to the free program, they were completely exhausted—especially Chris. Somehow, he rallied for the performance, and they earned two 6.0s for technical merit, and an astonishing seven (out of a possible nine) 6.0s for artistic impression! One of the judges, Pamela Davis, had once said she had never given a 6.0 and never would. On this November evening, she gave out two! Davis explains:

1. They were technically brilliant. 2. They have a beautiful soft knee with a rise and fall which is the essence of dance. 3. They have softness and

quietness on turns of high quality, with no scrapes or scratches. 4. The carriage was immaculately well held, without looking stiff and tight, relaxed without being limp. 5. The timing was flawless. 6. Their musical conception was superb, each dance interpreted that little bit differently from everyone else. 7. A rapport as deep as they achieved is so rare. 8. They were lost in the music and came over as one. And, if that were not enough, they've got a magic personality on the ice. I can watch "Mack and Mabel," and their "Summertime" for that matter, forever and never be bored. That's not so much rare as unprecedented in my experience.

Jayne and Chris were pleased to have won the British Championships again, the first time on their home turf since becoming world champions. But, never satisfied, they decided to go for the "gold star," the highest award a British skater can earn. It was a prize never before attempted by ice dancers. Previously, it had been won only by solo skaters. To win the gold star, Chris and Jayne would have to skate the past season's three compulsories, the present season's three compulsories, plus their short and long programs. And they only had forty-five minutes in which to do it! The test was nerve-racking and physically draining. It didn't help when they were asked to re-skate one program because of a technical problem with the sound system in the rink! Nevertheless, the partners passed the requirements and earned their highly prized gold stars.

As 1981 ended, Chris and Jayne had the European and World championships, a trail of perfect sixes, two gold stars, the M.B.E.s, and Jayne's distinction as the British press's "Sportswoman of the Year" to remember it by.

The European Championships were held in Lyons, France, in 1982. Unlike the previous year, when Chris and Jayne were viewed as up-and-comers in medal contention for the first time, now they were the favorites. They were watched closely, and there were interesting differences to note between them and the other couples. First of all, when they had practice sessions, they practiced their entire routine, uninterrupted, from start to finish. Most couples practiced in sections. The other thing they did differently from other couples was during competition. At the warm-up sessions before each section of competition, Chris and Jayne would take to the ice separately. Each would skate around, getting a feel for the surface. This was the way they normally began practices, and they felt, why do something different for the competition? Other couples were often a little startled—they were busy doing last-minute adjustments to their routines, skating that section just one more time, while Torvill and Dean were happy just skating around the ice by themselves.

Chris and Jayne's instincts were clearly right—for them, at least. This faith in their own judgment was another one of their strengths: They would not do what everyone else did; they would do what was right for them. And it worked. They won the three compulsories—a blues number (oddly enough, the short program was also a blues), the Yankee polka, and the Viennese waltz—even though Chris was fighting off another bout of stomach flu.

"Summertime" was a tremendous crowd pleaser. It was a dreamy, sensuous piece, full of languid swirls, slow dips, arms reaching out, and bodies curving around each other. It was both romantic and sad, full of love and love lost. It ended with a dramatic pose: Jayne lying across Christopher's back, their arms and legs stretched out in yearning. The effect was mesmerizing. The crowd and the judges thought so, too. Chris and Jayne were awarded three 5.9s for technical merit and three 6.0s for artistic impression.

So enthralled was England by their home team, that the BBC—the British Broadcasting Corporation, and the main source of television programming in Great Britain—actually delayed the nine o'clock news to broadcast "Mack and Mabel" live. The fans at home were not disappointed.

The scores were not disappointing either: three 6.0s and the rest 5.9s for technical merit, eight out of nine 6.0s for artistic impression! Once again, Torvill and Dean had done it. They were European champions for the second time and, along the way, had received an unprecedented fourteen 6.0s. How could they repeat such an incredible performance at the Worlds?

Betty Callaway made sure that they had a shot at it. She protected them from reporters and shielded them from their own publicity. She knew how important it was for her skaters to continue to train—not to rest on their laurels. They had become such big celebrities in Nottingham, that it was almost impossible for them to skate there without being interrupted. They had to retreat to Oberstdorf to ready themselves for the World Championships in Copenhagen, Denmark, in March 1982.

At a practice session for the Yankee polka in Copenhagen, Chris fell. He stood up, made a comic bow to the spectators, and skated on, but his fall did more than just interrupt a practice. It brought the skaters back down to earth—it showed them that anything could happen at any time.

When it was time for "Summertime," Torvill and Dean were in the lead, having won all three compulsories. This time, the crowd watched in hushed awe. The entire stadium was hushed as Chris and Jayne glided silently over the ice, playing, anguished lovers dancing the blues. A spell seemed to have enveloped them, and the audience, too. The couple barely remembers the performance, so entranced were they by the music, so involved in the emotion of the dance. The judges were equally transported by the seamless performance. Because of a change in the ISU rules, there were only seven judges that year. From them, Torvill and Dean received an incredible six 6.0s.

While doing the customary ISU tour, this time in the Soviet Union, some of the lucky skaters were given tickets to the famous Bolshoi Ballet. Jayne was thrilled to be seeing them at last, but, mysteriously, Christopher exchanged his ticket with someone who had tickets to the Moscow State Circus. Later in the tour, he acquired a French recording of a Broadway musical tune called *Barnum* that was currently also playing in London. It told the story of P. T. Barnum, the founder of the Barnum & Bailey Circus. When Torvill and Dean reached London, they went to see *Barnum*. Its star, Michael Crawford, a fan of the ice dancers, noticed them as he peeked at the audience before the show began, and invited them backstage afterwards. From this meeting grew the next Torvill and Dean sensation: their 1983 free dance to the music of *Barnum*.

After the astonishing success of "Mack and Mabel," Chris and Jayne were plagued by doubts and questions similar to those they had faced a year earlier. Had they peaked too soon? How could they possibly top the electrifying "Mack and Mabel"? Their answer, once again, lay in hard work and lots of experimentation, looking for help when they needed it, and seeking inspiration where they could find it. *Barnum* was just such an inspiration. Chris was excited by the possibilities of evoking a circus on ice, of communicating the easygoing, light-hearted pleasures of the big top at the skating rink.

Michael Crawford would prove an indispensable aide in this quest. Their first obstacle was the music: Most of the show's musical score included vocals, which were not allowed in ice-dancing music. Crawford arranged for a special recording session in which a scaled-down orchestra performed and connected the sections of the score that Chris and Jayne wanted for their program. He also sat rinkside and advised them on circus techniques and pantomime—it was his job to bring the proper theatricality to the piece.

As they set forth to painstakingly create another masterpiece, step by careful step, Chris was injured in a freak accident—he tripped on the sidewalk and broke a bone in his foot. The doctors told him he would have to stay off of it for a month. Chris, however, was back on the ice after twelve days. Amazingly, those twelve days were the longest Chris and Jayne had been off the ice in the history of their partnership!

The injury did allow them time to look for their short-program music, which that year had to be rock 'n' roll. Wanting to avoid any potential clichés, they searched long and hard for something danceable, usable, and unusual. They finally settled on a piece from an Andrew Lloyd Webber musical called *Song and Dance* that was actually a rock 'n' roll adaptation of a Paganini composition! With that decided, and with the injury behind them, they got to work on the 1982–1983 season.

For the last several years, Torvill and Dean's season had begun with the St. Ivel competition at Richmond. But now they felt that it was too early to unveil the new "Barnum" routine for two reasons: First, they did not feel quite ready—both their programs were difficult routines that required a great deal of preparation. Also, they did not want to skate the "Barnum" too soon in the season—it would lose its impact in the months between the St. Ivel and the Worlds. They agreed to skate an exhibition at the competition instead.

This decision gave Chris and Jayne plenty of extra time to perfect "Barnum." It also added an air of secrecy to their doings, which aroused the curiosity of the fans, the press, and their competitors. As a result, Chris and Jayne decided to hold a press conference the night before the British Championships to introduce the "Barnum" concept and to answer questions about it. They were so excited about its potential impact, though, that they decided not to practice it in public the morning of the competition.

They made waves at the British Championships even before they got to "Barnum." Chris,
Jayne, and Betty had decided that there were
numerous ways to be expressive in the compulsories without breaking the rules. They tried
subtle variations of their arm movements and
foot placements on each "circuit" (a trip around
the rink) of a given dance. Chris and Jayne were
still striving to make things better—not just for
themselves as skaters (although they wanted to
be better than their competitors, too!), but to
make the sport more artistic, more expressive,
more demanding.

Their rock 'n' roll short program was also a
sensation. With nonstop movement from beginning to end, it was very demanding physically,
both in the breathing and in the footwork. The
audience loved it, and Chris and Jayne felt they
could not have skated it any better.

"Barnum" went well by anyone else's standards, although Jayne had a tiny slip on the ice
and found herself worrying that her costume
would rip. They knew their performance was not
up to their usual standards. The judges awarded
them only one 6.0, the rest were 5.9s—wonderful scores, but not what they had been hoping
for. To keep this in perspective, it is helpful to
remember that before Torvill and Dean, 6.0s
were a rarity. There were judges who had *never*
given out a score that high. Within the space of
only two years, Torvill and Dean had become

accustomed to perfect scores—achieving anything less was a disappointment to them. Their
fans, however, were far from disappointed. The
audience loved "Barnum," and Chris and Jayne
received stacks of fan mail after winning the
British for the fifth straight year.

The couple was determined to work hard
between the British and the 1983 Europeans in
Dortmund, Germany, to make "Barnum" as
fool-proof and perfect as possible. In the mean-
time, they were bolstered by being chosen the
Sports Writers' Association's Team of the Year.
They were also elected the Team of the Year by
viewers of the BBC.

Another setback occurred while Chris and
Jayne were training in Oberstdorf, trying to
come up with a new opening for "Barnum."
They were practicing a new lift, where Jayne
would throw herself backwards while twisting in
the air and Chris would catch her while skating
backwards and twisting forward on the ice.
Their timing was off, and Jayne fell flat on her
back from about five feet off the ground. She
complained of numbness in her leg and said she
felt sick to her stomach. As Chris later recalled,
"I knew then she must have been severely
shaken because she's a brave girl who does not
make a fuss over anything. Whenever a new
move is suggested…she never ducks it on
grounds of safety…she does it without a second
thought."

Before Torvill and
Dean, 6.0s were a
rarity. But they
had become
accustomed to
perfect scores—
achieving
anything less was
a disappointment
to them.

Jayne felt better in a few days, and like a rider who has been thrown off a horse, she got right back on the ice and tried the new lift again. But the pain was too great—in her shoulder and her leg—and she knew she had to see a doctor. Luckily, x-rays revealed no broken bones, but she needed anti-inflammatory medication and *rest*. Of course, rest was the hardest thing for them to do, so anxious were they to prepare for the upcoming competition at Dortmund. For three days, Jayne stayed off the ice, and on the fourth day, under the watchful eye of her doctor, she laced up her skates. It took a full week for them to work up to a solid practice—four hours, still without any of the more strenuous moves. The next day, they were able to skate seven hours, and they felt sure they would be able to compete in the Europeans after all.

But the next day, Jayne fell again on that same lift. There was not as much pain as before, but it convinced them to change the move to something less troublesome. Unfortunately, that change came too late. Jayne's arm began to stiffen up over the next few days, making it virtually impossible for her to practice even the compulsories. With less than two weeks to go before the Europeans, Chris and Jayne had to face the inevitable: They would not be able to compete. They would not be ready, and, more importantly, they could not risk Jayne's health, not with a World title to defend.

This was not an easy decision, or an easy time, for them. With Jayne unable to skate, Chris was bored and anxious. Their normally placid relationship turned stormy. Once they had decided they would not compete at Dortmund, though, they were able to regain their composure and their good feelings. With the pressure off, they could relax and actually enjoy themselves for a few days! And with the saunas and swimming and treatments at the hospital, Jayne's arm began to feel better.

Chris and Jayne did not watch the Europeans. Unable to compete themselves, they did not want to know what their rivals were doing—or how they were doing, for that matter. And they did not want to find themselves moping about having missed the competition. Instead, they continued Jayne's treatments, and they continued to skate, avoiding complete run-throughs and their most vigorous movements. When the 1983 World Championships in Helsinki, Finland, were only two weeks away, they finally started to do their programs in their entirety.

Because they had missed the Europeans, Chris and Jayne arrived in Helsinki bubbling over with the desire to skate their absolute best. Chris was secretly striving for a 6.0 in the compulsories—something that no other ice dancer had yet achieved. Jayne was hoping her shoulder would hold up and that they would once again be world champions.

Their first compulsory was a snappy, quick-step, and they were soon in the lead. Their second compulsory was the Ravensburger waltz, and they got even higher marks for that. Their final compulsory, the Argentine tango, earned them a solid row of 5.9s. Chris remembers feeling that it was "the best compulsory we've ever done."

Going into the short and free programs, Chris and Jayne had a huge lead, but they still had something to prove. They wanted to show that they could top "Mack and Mabel," that they could get even higher scores, and that they had survived injury and come back even better. The short program, skated to Andrew Lloyd Webber's interpretation of Paganini, came first.

The rock 'n' roll went well—but not without a hitch. At one strategic moment, Jayne's satin skirt got caught between their two hands. It was on a tricky move, where Jayne was practically horizontal to the ice, held up only by Chris's hand. If they let go, Jayne would fall. If they left the skirt between their hands, Chris would not be able to spin Jayne back to him. Or the skirt might rip. With split-second, unspoken, mutual timing, they loosened their grip on each other's hands just the slightest bit, hoping the slippery material would simply slide out. It did, and the rest of the program went smoothly. Only a few judges noticed that tiny glitch, and it was not enough to diminish the audience's or the judges' enthusiasm. Torvill and Dean received seven 6.0s.

After a day off, it was time, at last, to skate "Barnum" for an international audience. The piece, full of acrobatics and clowning, pratfalls and tightrope walking, juggling and slide trombones, had a wonderful charm. It combined mime and mischief with the circus's trademark togetherness and sweetness. The audience started to applaud early and never stopped. The routine ends with a flip: Chris puts his head through Jayne's legs and flips her over his back. She lands with a flourish, and "Barnum" is over. No one could see the discreet strapping that held Jayne's shoulder together under her shiny white costume. And no one knew the bumpy road that led to those four minutes of unbridled perfection on the ice.

After a minute or two, the scores came up: straight 5.9s for technical merit. Next up on the board, for artistic impression, the marks that shook the ice-dancing world: nine 6.0s in a row. It had never happened before. Jayne shrieked with surprise and happiness. Chris kissed her in gratitude and relief.

The high of their Helsinki victory lasted only until Chris and Jayne set their sights on their future. As usual, Chris had been thinking ahead. The two had warmed up to Ravel's "Bolero" for several years. A deceptively repetitive piece of music, it has the same driving beat throughout.

It is one long crescendo that starts out as a wisp of melody and gains strength and momentum until its dramatic, sudden ending. Chris now felt that it was time to use the piece in competition. "Bolero" had an entirely different feel from the upbeat free programs they had performed in the last two years. It was dramatic, romantic, and sensuous, but also tragic. Chris made up a story to tell with the skating: Two doomed lovers, fated never to be together, climb a mountain and hurl themselves off, preferring death to-gether to life apart. Very melodramatic stuff indeed, but the story's purpose was to help Chris choreograph the piece. Watching them skate, you did not need to know the specifics. You could feel the love and the anguish, simply by seeing them move.

The short program that year was a *paso doble*—and Chris and Jayne decided to exploit its bullfighting origins to the hilt. They made Chris a matador and Jayne his cape! As odd as this may sound, it was a brilliant decision, allowing Chris to fling Jayne all over the ice and show off an uncharacteristically "haughty" attitude.

Oberstdorf was once again the primary site of their summer labors. They had already decided that this would be their last year of competitive skating. After the Olympics, there would be no more competitive heights to be scaled, only artistic ones. Chris and Jayne felt that the only way to pursue those artistic dreams was to go

professional, to create ice dances without the
constraints imposed by the rigid rules of the
ISU. Many people assumed that they would
make a lot of money by turning pro and perhaps
that was part of their motivation. But in interview after interview, it was clear that Chris and
Jayne wanted the freedom to express themselves
fully on ice.

Before they could do that, there was the 1983–
1984 season, and the Olympics that it would
bring. Just as they had done the year previous, they
decided to meet with the press the night before the
British competitions to introduce their programs.
This time, though, they decided to skate the program for the press as well. The British press was so
stunned, they did not know how to describe what
they had seen. There were some concerns about
the legality of certain moves. And more than
anything, people were now dying to see how it
would be judged.

As it turned out, the judgments in the competition were very favorable. For technical merit,
their marks were all 5.9s, for artistic impression:
six 6.0s and the other three 5.9s. Clearly the
judges did not think any of the moves were
illegal. They loved the program. Chris and Jayne
had garnered their sixth consecutive British
Championship.

The British Champions now moved on to
Budapest, Hungary, where Chris and Jayne had
long ago trained with Regoeczy and Sallay.

Although they were returning to the Europeans after a year's absence, it would not be a simple coronation ceremony. Torvill and Dean would have to earn their title, as they had every year for the last three years.

The compulsories showed Torvill and Dean at their usual, impeccable, best. Chris finally realized his dream of receiving a 6.0 on a compulsory in international competition. In fact, they earned two! The *paso doble* was a rousing success with the audience, the other skaters, and most of the judges. (Bestemianova, of the rival B & B Soviet duo, told them it was "so beautiful I could not free myself from the memory of it all day.") The *paso doble* begins with Jayne draping her hands over Chris's shoulder, the cape ready to be whipped out and waved. Chris drags her along the ice, then boldly hurls her around the rink. It ends with him dropping her to the ground, where she spins to a halt, face down on the ice. It is a tremendously exciting, athletic, and masterful piece, aided by a dramatic *paso doble* by Rimsky-Korsakov. The technical scores were all 5.9s—except for a 5.8 from a Czech judge and an incredible 5.6 from the Soviet judge. The crowd booed. Artistic marks: six 6.0s, three 5.9s. That was better—but what did the Soviet judge's low score mean? Were there illegal moves in the *paso doble?* Or was it a kind of warning about possible illegal moves in "Bolero"?

We will never know the answers to those questions because, when "Bolero" finally premiered, the judges were completely seduced. The pair received nothing but 5.9s and 6.0s, thus regaining their European title. They now looked forward to the ultimate event of their amateur-skating careers: the 1984 Olympic Winter Games in Sarajevo, Yugoslavia.

Sarajevo is now a battleground, but at that time, the country was still holding together a delicate peace. Its people, harmonious and relaxed, opened their capital city with hospitality and joy to the rest of the world. Chris was honored to be the British team member chosen to carry his country's flag—the Union Jack—in the opening procession. They prepared, they concentrated, they waited.

The compulsories were first, of course, and they received not two, but three, perfect scores

Their "Bolero" routine at the 1984 Olympics earned Chris and Jayne the highest scores ever awarded in ice-dancing competition.

Jayne and Chris enjoy the adulation from the Olympic crowd after the scores for "Bolero" were posted.

for their Westminster waltz! Not everything else, however, would go as smoothly and effortlessly. In their gorgeous, dramatic *paso doble*, Jayne touched her hand down on the ice for a split second—a tiny mistake, but for them highly unusual. It was enough to earn them less than unanimous 6.0s—*only* four, but still enough to keep them in the lead.

And then, "Bolero." The audience was silent, transfixed. Chris and Jayne's bodies swayed to the music as they skated effortlessly in and around each other. They wove a spell that was not broken until their final fall to the ice, representing the lovers flinging themselves down into the abyss. The audience was on their feet at once. They clapped without end, as if hoping for an encore, unwilling to stop offering their approval. A shower of bouquets fell to the ice. Jayne skated around, trying to catch them all, and was unable to make it to the customary seats where skaters normally watch for their scores. She heard a roar from the crowd and looked up. Not the straight 5.9s they had received at the Worlds for technical merit—no, better: they had three 6.0s! A pause. Then the scores for artistic impression flashed onto the scoreboard: nine perfect 6.0s—an Olympic first and last. The ultimate score at the ultimate sporting event. It was the dream beyond all dreams. Jayne beamed and buried her head in Christopher's shoulder. A wave to the crowd, and they were into the history books. They were now officially the best ice dancers ever.

As Chris walked by a British reporter, he was asked, "How did it go?" Without missing a beat, he replied, "All right."

The Professional Years

"As a skater [Jayne] is the perfect partner,

for me at least. Much of the

originality of our programs may come

from me but that is only because Jayne

makes it possible."

—*Christopher Dean*

The World Championship competition that followed the Olympics *was* a coronation. The 6.0s rained down like the bouquets: there were seven in the compulsories, nine for the magnificent *paso doble*, four for technical merit, and nine for artistic expression with "Bolero." They skated their fourth and final World Championship in Ottawa, Canada, where, just six years earlier, Betty Callaway had first noticed the "new British couple."

Chris and Jayne had set a new standard for all ice dancers to follow. The sport would never be the same again. What made Torvill and Dean so special? First, they brought a real dance sensibility to ice skating. They treated their programs as complete entities, whether telling a story or just evoking a mood, that could stand on their own. Their free dance was no longer just a showcase for skating talents, performed exclusively for the judges, but a treat to be savored by the audience, whether or not they knew anything about the technical aspects of skating.

Torvill and Dean also brought an extreme sensitivity for music to the sport. Not only did they make bold choices in their musical selections, but they also integrated their movements with the music better than anyone else. As Jayne once said in a magazine interview, "A lot of people don't understand about fitting all this to music. But we look upon a piece of music as a picture; we see it and not hear it."

Torvill and Dean also introduced inventive, thoughtful choreography to ice dancing. Christopher Dean is a brilliant choreographer, but not just because he comes up with pretty moves. His choreography is remarkable because it suits both the music and the skaters so well. He does not try to force his "vision" onto a routine, nor does he start with a "concept" and hope that the music will go along with it. For Christopher, the idea for any routine always begins with the music. The final ingredient that enables him to successfully realize the music's vision is that he and Jayne skate so well.

In light of their many ground-breaking, show-stopping, crowd-pleasing numbers, it is easy to lose sight of the fact that they are also technically excellent skaters and athletes. It is their superb technique that allowed their choreography to happen, not the other way around. Talking about technique helps to define Jayne's invaluable contribution to the partnership. Not only did she bring emotional stability, a thirst for perfection, and the guts to practice a move over and over, she also brought excellent, fearless technique. As Chris told John Hennessy, an early biographer:

> As a skater she is the perfect partner, for me at least. Much of the originality of our programs may come from me but that is only because Jayne makes it possible. She seems almost to float on the ice with a lovely, soft action and when I want her to go in a particular way she moves with no apparent effort on her part and little persuasion on mine. It just seems to happen, so much so that I tend to take her for granted. It is when I am trying to help another girl that I really realize my luck.
> We seem, too, to have a telepathic understanding. Some people say that we are so perfectly tuned into the same wavelength that if one of us makes a mistake the other can instinctively cover it and it will go unnoticed. It may happen but I am not conscious of it. She is such a superlative technician that I know she will always be there, exactly where I want her, at precisely the split second.

"We look upon a piece of music as a picture; we see it and not hear it."

After Chris and Jayne won the 1984 Worlds,
their future had to wait until the inevitable ISU
tour was over. During the tour, Chris and Jayne
were asked to dance "Bolero" over and over,
with encore after encore. Audiences knew that
an era in amateur ice dancing was coming to an
end. For their part, Chris and Jayne were looking forward to a professional future that would
push the limits of ice dancing, and their own
abilities, even further. Hard workers to the end,
they set about forming a company and preparing
their first professional tour as soon as they returned from the ISU tour.

For a skater, going professional after having
spent years performing as an amateur creates a
series of contradictions. On the one hand, touring makes one much more accessible to fans. On
the other hand, a pro is not in the public eye as
much as when he or she was competing, with
the constant reporting in the newspapers and
live coverage on television. And while competitive skating is supposed to be more difficult and
exacting, an amateur is performing only infre-
quently, and then, for only two or four minutes
at a time. Professionals must perform *every*
night, often for one or two hours at a time. For
Chris and Jayne's first tour, they skated every
program that had made them famous, from
"Mack and Mabel" to "Bolero"—the routines,
however, were not spread out over three years,
but rather, done in the space of an evening.

Their first professional tour took them to New Zealand and Australia. As 1984 came to a close, they were voted BBC Sports Personalities of the Year and won their first World Professional Ice Skating Championship. Soon after that, they started to put together their own company of skaters for their first professional world tour.

That tour would take them through 1985 and 1986, and it would introduce newly choreographed works, many of them longer and bolder than anything they could have done as amateurs. They strove to make their ice shows something more than the traditional showy revue. As part of this ongoing quest to increase the "dance" in ice dancing, Chris started to work on "Fire and Ice," an evening-long ice-dance performance that was ultimately taped for the BBC and broadcast in 1986. It was later released on videotape. The year 1986 also brought their world tour to a close, and in 1987, they toured the United States with the Ice Capades. A glowing review of that collaboration said, "With Torvill and Dean, it's the way they work together that's so extraordinary. Dean is an exemplary partner. He barely seems to touch Torvill as he wraps her near his own body or tosses her into airborne configurations...Their conceptual originality and smooth-as-silk execution are heightened by the implicit relationship: man and woman conquering time and space together." Three

"It's the way they work together that's so extraordinary. Dean is an exemplary partner. He barely seems to touch Torvill as he wraps her near his own body ..."

Chris and Jayne starred in a traveling ice show in 1985 and 1986.

years after turning pro, it was clear they had not lost their touch.

After the Ice Capades, Torvill and Dean started preparations for another world tour, this time with a cast of Soviet skaters. Meanwhile, they began to pursue outside interests as well—something that had been impossible for them in the past. Chris, always high-strung, became addicted to speed—in the form of auto racing. (In fact, at the 1984 Winter Olympics, he persuaded a bobsled team to let him have a run down the course, just for the sheer exhilaration of it!) He took driving lessons, and soon was competing in celebrity events.

He also started to coach an up-and-coming ice dancing couple, Isabelle and Paul Duchesnay. Originally from Canada, but now skating for France, they were a brother-and-sister team who had trained at the same complex in Oberstdorf as Torvill and Dean. Considered very avant-garde for ice dancers, their style was somewhat in the Torvill and Dean mode, but even more so. Christopher Dean was choreographing their programs, so, naturally, they were constantly pushing at the limits of what was allowable and expected in competition.

Unfortunately for Chris and his new protégés, the ISU was clamping down, making the ice-dancing rules more rigid and restrictive than they had been during Torvill and Dean's heyday. In the wake of "Bolero," ice-dancing couples everywhere had been flinging themselves down on the ice, emoting wildly without bothering to skate well, too. Chris and Jayne had "earned" the right to bend the rules. They had solid technique underneath the emotions. Such was not always the case with Torvill and Dean imitators, and the ISU went after them. "Everyone in skating realized it," said Scott Hamilton, the U.S. gold medalist at the 1984 Olympics. "Torvill and Dean were sensational, just remarkable. But what followed got silly. Even talented skaters were doing dumb things." The ISU banned dragging a skater by his or her skate (a move T&D had used in "Barnum" and "Bolero"). It also banned any falls to the ice (the trademark finish to "Bolero" and, to some extent, the *paso doble*).

In 1988, "Torvill and Dean and the Russian All-Stars" started to tour the globe. When they got to the United States in 1989, something very special happened. Jayne met an American sound engineer named Phil Christensen who was helping with the tour. He asked her out on a date and within months, they were engaged and then married. Did this alter the delicate, intimate balance between Chris and Jayne, famous for their steamy on-ice relationship? Apparently not. Luckily for Jayne, Phil was used to the performer's life: As a sound engineer for Phil Collins and Genesis, among other musical groups, Christensen knew all about the demands of touring and the work required to stay on top of your craft. He knew not to be jealous of Jayne and Chris's on-ice intimacy, recognizing it as *performance.*

The year 1990 also brought Torvill and Dean another World Professional Championship, new honors as American World Professional Skaters, and a British tour that outsold the Rolling Stones! In 1991, the BBC show "Omnibus" broadcast a program highlighting Christopher's choreography—it was the highest-rated "Omnibus" episode of the season. Also in that year, Torvill and Dean were invited to tour Australia as guests of the South Australian government.

Meanwhile, Chris was continuing to choreograph and coach the Duchesnays, who, in 1991, won the World Championships in Munich, Germany. In the wake of that success, Chris and Isabelle Duchesnay decided to get married. Unfortunately, it was to be only a short-lived marriage. As Christopher said after their 1993 divorce, "We weren't compatible and should never have married, but sometimes you don't see the realities until too late."

It was right around this time that the International Olympic Committee (IOC) made a decision that would have a profound effect on Torvill and Dean. The committee decided to allow professional ice skaters to compete in the Winter Games. They also moved the 1996 Games forward two years—to 1994—so that the summer and winter Olympics would alternate in two-year intervals.

In 1992, Chris and Jayne were invited to a celebration of the International Skating Union's 100th anniversary in Davos, Switzerland. While they were there, they heard about the IOC's rule change. Jayne, apparently, thought nothing of it, but Chris, naturally, saw a challenge he had to meet—and beat. On the train ride back from the party, Chris said to Jayne, "Do you think we should try it next year?" Jayne was not even sure what he meant at first, but once she had mulled it over, she agreed to give it a try. As she said, "When I began thinking about how many minutes of performing we would have in competition versus how many minutes we would have on our current tour, it started to look pretty good. The timing was right: 1996 would have been too late, but at the 1994 Olympics, Jayne would be 36, and Christopher, 35—not *too* terribly old. They were in terrific shape, in some ways in even better shape than when they had competed before—performing eight two-hour shows a week builds up a huge stamina. They knew too, that their professional careers would be ending soon: Jayne was married and wanted to have children. Chris had recently fallen in love with American figure-skating world champion Jill Trenary, and they would need time to build a life together. Torvill and Dean could not tour forever.

Why not go out with a bang?

The Comeback and the Controversy

"...We love to go out and

perform...it's part of us."

—*Christopher Dean*

In March of 1993, Torvill and Dean announced their return to competitive skating. At a press conference, they talked about their reasons. Chris told the media: "Through our professional life we have developed, learnt more, matured. We still believe we have the ability, and we love to go out and perform. At the end of the day we're exhibitionists. It's part of us and it's something we want to do, to be out there in front of an audience performing." When asked how they felt about the restrictions that had been placed on ice dancing during the

90

intervening ten years, Jayne said: "There had
to be restrictions to keep it to the point where
skaters can be judged. Because we've been professionals we've had absolutely none, and it's not
a challenge. We have to conform."

As part of their "re-education," Torvill and
Dean talked to judges and others in the skating
hierarchy to find out what the judges were looking for at that time. Were they still so strict?
Had the rules loosened up? What did the ISU
want? They came away with a very strong feeling
that the ISU wanted skaters to emphasize
traditional ice-dancing techniques: impeccable
footwork, partners skating together in absolute
synchronicity, no tricks, no stunts—just skating.

Throughout their skating careers, Chris and
Jayne had been drawn to the image created by
the American dance team of Fred Astaire and
Ginger Rogers. They had based exhibition routines on this concept in their amateur days and
had performed Fred-and-Ginger numbers in
their professional shows. As the ultimate ballroom dancers, Fred and Ginger seemed to glide
across those glossy floors in the movies as if they
were on ice. They were classy, smooth, and most
importantly, very, very good. It seemed fitting
somehow to conjure up this inspirational duo,
these symbols of ballroom dance at its best, for
their farewell competition. They chose "Let's
Face the Music and Dance," a number performed by Fred and Ginger and written by

Irving Berlin, for their long program. "The piece takes us back to social dancing, to the rhythms of the ballroom—fox-trot, waltz, and tango—with a couple of surprises. We've known the music for a long time, but it was question of finding the right vehicle for it. We believe it is the way the ISU wants ice dancing to go."

Ten years after turning pro, they returned to rehearsing four hours a day, six days a week on their compulsories (the Starlight waltz and the blues), their short program (the rumba), and the all-important free dance. This time, they trained at the Bladerunner Arena in England's Milton Keynes. Once again, they asked Betty Callaway to help, and enlisted Bobby Thompson, another

Ten years after becoming professional skaters, Chris and Jayne began training for an Olympic comeback.

member of the team from the "old days," plus a director they had worked with on a number of tours, Andris Toppe. They brought in an arranger to get the Big-Band sound of "Let's Face the Music and Dance" exactly right. They consulted with top costume designers to create the perfect three costumes: one for the compulsories, one for the short program, and one for the long program. They used video cameras to record their every move—and to perfect it. But most of all, they worked themselves harder than ever.

Understanding that the ISU was looking for flawless technique and a return to "real" dancing, they designed a free program that had extremely intricate footwork but would look effortless and smooth. In the first minute of the new free dance, they did more steps, more moves, and more footwork than they had in all of "Bolero."

In the ten years since they had last competed, the schedule of events had changed. The British Championships were now held in January, instead of November. The location of the British competition had changed, too: to Sheffield from hometown Nottingham. But one thing that had not changed was the anticipation surrounding a new Torvill and Dean free dance. Once again, they held a preview performance for the press on the eve of the competition. The press were suitably impressed, except for a few veteran journalists who had covered Chris and Jayne's amateur career the first time around. Yes, the footwork was dazzling and beautifully executed, but then some thought there was something lacking—that trademark spark.

The judges at the British Championships did not agree. They loved all that Torvill and Dean had to offer them. Their marks for the Starlight waltz averaged 5.7; for the blues, 5.8. Their rumba—which, like "Summertime" those many years ago, was skated at the slowest possible tempo—was a tour de force. Haughty, sexy, striking, it brought down the house with its bold moves danced to a moody trumpet melody. The judges gave it five 5.9s and four 6.0s. Torvill and Dean were back!

"Let's Face the Music and Dance" did not let them down. For technical merit, they received eight 5.9s and one 6.0; for artistic impression, the Torvill and Dean trademark: a row of perfect 6.0s. Ten years later, they were back on the podium, gold medalists again, and British champs for the seventh time!

It was just the boost they would need to get them to the European Championships in Copenhagen, where the competition would begin in earnest. And, just like old times, their main competition would be two Soviet couples: Maia Usova and Alexandr Zhulin, reigning world champions, and the young, up-and-coming Oksana Gritschuk and Evgeny Platov. Usova and Zhulin were known for their expressive elegance; Gritschuk and Platov, for their youthful exuberance. Torvill and Dean were by no means a sure thing for first place.

In fact, after the first compulsory, Chris and Jayne were in third place. After the second compulsory, they were tied for second place with Gritschuk and Platov, behind Usova and Zhulin. Torvill and Dean needed high marks for their short program, the rumba, to ensure that they would be in contention for the gold by the time the free dance rolled around. Their marks for composition (similar to technical merit) ranged from an incredible low of 5.5 to a more predictable 5.9. The audience hissed in disapproval. The marks for presentation were better: only one 5.8, six 5.9s, and two 6.0s. They were tied for first with the world champs, Usova and Zhulin. Gritschuk and Platov were in third place.

Everything now depended on the free dance. Usova and Zhulin, with a light, lyrical program that showed them at their elegant best, skated first of the top three couples. They received five 5.7s, three 5.8s, and one 5.9 for technical merit. The scores were high but not unbeatable. For artistic impression, their scores got higher: two 5.8s; the rest, 5.9s. Could Torvill and Dean squeak through?

Chris and Jayne were up next, to be followed by Gritschuk and Platov. They skated into the the rink, back into the thick of international competition, right into the moment when they were forced to "face the music and dance." The crowd was glad to welcome them back. They shrieked when the pair took the ice, they clapped along to the music, and they applauded long and hard at the end. The judges weighed in with three 5.7s, five 5.8s, and a 5.9 for technical merit, better than Usova and Zhulin. What they saw for artistic impression, however, left them short: six 5.9s, and the rest, 5.8s. Usova and Zhulin were ahead. At that point, Chris and Jayne waited only to see whether they would end up in second or third place. Where they ended up would depend on how the judges scored the final pair, Gritschuk and Platov, who performed a rock 'n' roll piece, that seemed, to Chris and Jayne, to be full of the kind of jazzy pyrotechnics that they had been instructed to avoid. And yet, this couple received the highest scores of all: seven 5.9s, and two 5.8s for technical; two 5.8s, four 5.9s, and a pair of 6.0s for artistic. Because Gritschuk and Platov had been third coming into the free dance, it was not clear right away who would win the championship.

The scoring is figured as follows: The winner is not determined by just adding up the scores, decimal points and all, to see who has the highest total number of points. At the end of any given section, the judges scores are examined to see who they have placed highest (first place), second highest (second place), and so on. Seven judges put Gritschuk and Platov in first place for the free dance, but since the couple had been a distant third for the rest of the competition, this was not enough to earn them the gold. First place would now go either to Torvill and Dean or Usova and Zhulin, depending on which of them received the most *second-place* rankings from the judges (the first-place rankings had effectively been thrown out since Gritschuk and Platov could not win due to their poor performance in the rest of the competition). In this odd system, the important thing is to have the most second-place rankings.

As a result of this tortuous process, Torvill and Dean became European champions once again. They were thrilled to have the title, but there was a bittersweet taste to their victory. They knew they had won due to a peculiarity in the scoring rules. It was clear to them that the judges were not happy with their free dance. With only weeks until the Olympics in Norway, Chris and Jayne made a decision: They would gut their free dance and completely rework it. Trying to follow the new ice-dancing dictum by emphasizing pure dance had been a mistake. They had clearly been outdone by a flashy rock 'n' roll piece that was a crowd pleaser and not exactly an example of ballroom-style restraint.

With the pressure on, the rehearsals were tense. Chris, feeling betrayed by the advice he had been given and impatient with the process of reinventing eighty percent of their free dance, sometimes took his frustrations out on Jayne, who, on at least one occasion, left the ice in tears. Even Jayne, the ever-placid, forgiving one, could only take so much of the infamous Christopher Dean temper.

They worked furiously to add more razzle-dazzle, more show-biz, more pizzazz. They snuck in a few moves from their famous routines of the past as a kind of inside joke and to save time. They added some lovely, surprising role-reversals: At one point, Chris lifts Jayne into the air; right afterwards, she lifts him. At another point, he makes a little leap that imitates a leap of Jayne's. They kept a lot of the footwork, they never lost the finesse, and they most definitely added flash.

In Norway, their performance in the compulsories disappointed—and bewildered—them. Why, when they were skating as well as they ever had, were they receiving lower scores? A suspicion started to take root among the ice-dancing insiders that the IOC had allowed professionals to compete—perhaps to increase interest in the sport—but that the judges were going into the competitions preju-diced against them. This accusation would be repeated throughout the Olympics, since all of the professional skaters were consistently scored lower than the amateurs against whom they were competing.

After the compulsories, Torvill and Dean
were in third place. They would have to win the
short program to even be eligible for the gold
medal. They skated the rumba very beautifully.
The audience adored it. Thankfully, the judges
did, too: four 5.9s, and the rest, 5.8s for composition; seven 5.9s and two Olympic 6.0s for
presentation!

At last, it had come to four minutes of putting blade to ice to determine whether or not
they would take home another Olympic gold
medal. Torvill and Dean would skate second-to-
last, after Usova and Zhulin and just before
Gritschuk and Platov.

Usova and Zhulin skated very, very well.
They received a row of 5.8s and one 5.9 for
technical merit and a row of 5.9s punctuated
with three 5.8s for artistic impression. Now it
was Torvill and Dean's turn. They took their
places in the center ring, ready to give it their all.
After ten years away, after six grueling months of
preparation, after the panic-stricken two weeks
of revamping their entire long program, they
had nothing to lose. They had no choice but
to skate all out.

Their performance was pure magic, as anyone
who witnessed it will attest. It was cheeky, ener-
getic, adorable, and wonderfully snazzy. They
skated it with confidence and flair, with an ease
and confidence that no younger skater could
fake. The routine ended on a high, with Jayne

flipping over Chris's head, just as she had all those years ago in "Barnum." The crowd went wild. The skaters' faces were filled with relief and triumph—it was obvious that they felt they had skated as well as they possibly could.

The judges felt differently. Expecting a satisfying string of sixes, Olympic sports fans in Lillehammer were shocked by the numbers that flashed on the board. For technical merit:

5.8 5.7 5.9 5.8 5.7 5.7 5.7 5.6 5.7

For artistic impression:

5.8 5.9 6.0 5.9 5.9 5.9 5.8 5.9 5.9

It would not be enough for the gold.

In fact, the gold medal went to Gritschuk and Platov and their flashy rock 'n' roll program. Usova and Zhulin received the silver medal, leaving Torvill and Dean to receive the bronze. What had happened? Why were the scores so blatantly low when many commentators, sports journalists, and fans felt theirs was clearly the best free dance of the competition? Some thought maybe the final back flip was considered illegal. (It is a violation of the rules for the man to lift the woman above his shoulders.) But, as Christopher pointed out, it was not a lift—he did not pick her up, but used gravity to send her over his head. When the move begins, he is bending down, making her no higher than shoulder-level to begin with.

If the judges were being scrupulous about rules infractions, how could they have ignored

Although their skating seemed better than ever, Chris and Jayne left the 1994 Olympics with only the bronze.

the many times Gritschuk and Platov had separated, sometimes for ten seconds, when only five seconds is allowed? Again, rumors circulated about an unspoken prejudice against professionals in the competition.

After the Lillehammer performance, Torvill and Dean's millions of fans in Great Britain were up in arms. Headlines screamed: "Gold Robbery," "As Good as Gold," "Robbed of Gold," "Viewers' Fury at T&D 'fix,'" and "Was It Rigged?"

Jayne and Chris felt equally bewildered. After the compulsories, Chris had said, "It has been harder than we thought, and we were deflated because we skated hard. If we had known before what we know now, we would not have come back because of the mental stress of everything. We are positive about what we can do, but it's not a question of getting to the line faster than someone else. It's about impressing nine judges and sensing what their general mood is." In light of what was to come, these words seem almost prophetic.

Gracious as always, they beamed from the podium during the medal ceremony. Ambitious people like Chris and Jayne are driven by a desire to be the best—and bronze is not *the* best. But to return to competitive skating after ten years—now much older than all the competitors—and still win the hearts of millions all over again and end up third in the *world* is not so bad after all.

"If we had known before what we know now, we would not have come back because of the mental stress of everything."

Together, Chris and Jayne remain the most successful and influential ice-dancing pair ever.

For Chris and Jayne, Lillehammer would be the end of the road. They would not go on to the World Championships a month later. They had skated their best at the Olympics, and they decided to leave it at that.

*　*　*

That is not the end of the Torvill and Dean story, though it is the end of the drama—for now. As his final act in Lillehammer, Chris got down on his knee and proposed to Jill Trenary. They were married in October 1994.

After he was settled into his new marriage, Chris was ready to dive headlong into the future. Chris and Jayne immediately set about assembling a new group of skaters for a "Face the Music" world tour, which will probably be their last. It includes the two Olympic show-stoppers—the rumba and the Fred-and-Ginger routine—as well as some lovely, adventurous works that show Torvill and Dean will remain the classiest act on ice for a while to come. They are still so young that their lives could include many more milestones and achievements. Will Jayne have children? Will Chris continue to choreograph? Will they become coaches for the next hot, young duo in ice dancing? Anything seems possible for these working-class kids from Nottingham who have the drive, the vision, and the unique bond to make miracles happen on an oval of ice.

Glossary

artistic impression The scores that a skater or skaters receive for their interpretation of a dance or for performing a long program.

circuit A complete trip around the ice-skating rink; a specific tour or set of competitions in which skaters regularly participate.

compulsories In ice dancing, the dances and the steps that must be performed to specific music in competitions.

exhibition An ice-skating performance that is not judged.

figure skating A form of ice skating performed alone or as a couple in which athletics are emphasized.

free dance A part of competitive skating in which skaters are allowed to select their own music and freely choreograph their routines.

ice dancing Ice skating in couples to ballroom music. In competitions, ice dancers must perform a set of predetermined steps to particular types of music.

pairs skating A form of ice skating in which a couple demonstrates their athletic ability with throws, lifts, spins and holds.

rumba A ballroom dance of Cuban origin that is noted for its hip movements; music for this dance.

salchow A jump in which the figure skater leaps from the back inside edge of one skate making a complete revolution of the body in the air and lands on the back outside edge of the other skate.

short program In ice dancing, a short, originally choreographed routine that is skated to a preselected type of music. It is also called the Original Program.

sit-spin A spin that is performed on one skate in which the skater slowly squats down into a sitting position with the other leg extended out in front.

technical merit The scores that a skater or skaters receive for attempting to skillfully demonstrate specific techniques.

triple axle A jump performed by a skater leaping from the front outer edge of one skate into the air to make three-and-a-half rotations of the body and landing on the back outer edge of the other skate.

Bibliography

Copley-Graves, Lynn. *Figure Skating History: The Evolution of Dance on Ice.* Columbus, OH: Platero Press, 1992.

Hennessy, John. *Torvill and Dean.* London: David and Charles, 1983.

Hilton, Christopher. *Torvill and Dean: The Full Story.* Somerset, England: Oxford Illustrated Press, 1994.

"Jayne Torvill and Christopher Dean: Ice Capades." *Dancemagazine*, May 1988.

"Sensuality and Ice Magic." *Time*, Nov. 24, 1986.

"To Finish on a High." *Newsweek*, Feb. 21, 1994.

"Torvill and Dean: A Class Act Returns to the Olympic Arena to Save Their Floundering Sport." *Life*, Feb. 1994.

"Torvill and Dean and the Russian All-Stars." *Dancemagazine*, Jan. 1990.

Torvill, Jayne, Dean, Christopher, with Wilson, Neil. *Torvill and Dean: Fire on Ice.* London: Weidenfeld and Nicolson, 1994.

Further Reading

Arnold, Caroline. *The Olympic Winter Games.* New York: Watts, 1991.

Coffey, Wayne. Katarina Witt: Magical Skater. Woodbridge, CT: Blackbirch, 1992.

Copley-Graves, Lynn. *Figure Skating History: The Evolution of Dance on Ice.* Columbus, OH: Platero Press, 1992.

Jarrett, William. *Timetables of Sports History: The Olympic Games.* New York: Facts On File, 1990.

Knight, Theodore. *The Olympic Games.* San Diego: Lucent Books, 1991.

Savage, Jeff. *Kristi Yamaguchi.* New York: Macmillian, 1993.

Skating. Irving, TX: Boy Scouts of America, 1983.

Trenary, Jill. *The Day I Skated for the Gold.* New York: Simon and Schuster, 1989.

Chronology

October 7, 1957 Jayne Torvill is born in Nottingham.
July 27, 1958 Christopher Dean is born in Nottingham.
1970 Torvill, with partner Michael Hutchinson, wins British Junior Pairs championships and is second in Senior Pairs.
1971 Torvill and Hutchinson win British Senior Pairs.
1972 Dean, with partner Sandra Elson, wins British Primary Dance Championships. Torvill and Hutchinson place eighteenth in the European Pairs championship.
1974 Dean and Elson win British Junior Dance Championship and place sixth in Seniors.
1975 Janet Sawbridge becomes coach to Torvill and Dean.
1976 Torvill and Dean win the Sheffield Trophy and the Northern Championship; and at St. Gervais. They place second at Oberstdorf, and fourth at the British Championships.
1977 Torvill and Dean win at Oberstdorf and come in third at the British Championships.
1978 Torvill and Dean come in ninth at the European championships and eleventh at the Worlds. Betty Callaway becomes their coach. They win the John Davis Trophy and the British Championships.
1979 Torvill and Dean place sixth in the Europeans; eighth in the Worlds; win the British Championships; come in second in the Rotary Watches Competition; and second in the NHK Competition in Tokyo.
1980 The duo places fourth in Europeans; wins the Worlds; wins the British; and are awarded the MBE.
1982 Torvill and Dean win the Europeans, the Worlds, and the British Championships.

1983 The pair wins the Worlds and the British Championships.

1984 Torvill and Dean win the Europeans, the Olympics, and the Worlds.

1985 The duo turns professional and makes their first world tour. They win the World Professional Championships.

1986 Torvill and Dean make their first television special: "Fire and Ice."

1987 The pair tours as guests of the Ice Capades.

1988 Torvill and Dean make their second world tour with the Russian All-Stars.

1990 The duo wins the World Professional Championships. Torvill marries Phil Christensen.

1991 Torvill and Dean tour Australia. Dean choreographs for the Duchesnays, who win the Worlds. Dean marries Isabelle Duchesnay.

1993 The pair tour the United States. They decide to compete again. Dean divorces Duchesnay.

1994 Torvill and Dean win the British Championships and the Europeans. They place third at the Olympics. Dean marries Jill Trenary. Torvill and Dean begin a world tour.

Index